THE JULIO-CLAUDIAN EMPERORS
AD 14-70

Current and forthcoming titles in the Classical World Series

Classical World Series

THE JULIO-CLAUDIAN EMPERORS: AD 14-70

Thomas Wiedemann

Bristol Classical Press

General Editor: John H. Betts
Series Editor: Michael Gunningham

First published in 1989 by
Bristol Classical Press
an imprint of
Gerald Duckworth & Co. Ltd
The Old Piano Factory
48 Hoxton Square, London N1 6PB

Reprinted with amendments 1995, 1997

A catalogue record for this book is available
from the British Library

ISBN 1-85399-117-1

Available in USA and Canada from:
Focus Information Group
PO Box 369
Newburyport
MA 01950

Printed in Great Britain by
Arrowhead Books Ltd, Reading, Berkshire

Contents

Acknowledgements

The picture of Roman political history from Tiberius to Vespasian which is proffered here will be presented in greater detail in chapters 6 and 7 of the forthcoming new edition of volume X of the *Cambridge Ancient History*. I would like to thank David Braund, Andrew Lintott, Jürgen Malitz and Brian Warmington for their comments on a draft of those chapters; and Barbara Levick for her many helpful suggestions for the present volume.

TEJW

List of Illustrations

STEMMA I: DESCENDANTS OF AUGUSTUS AND LIVIA

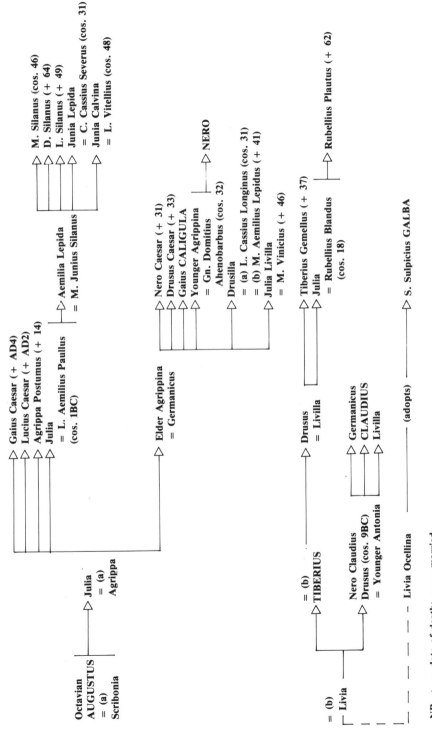

NB. + = date of death; = = married

STEMMA II: DESCENDANTS OF AUGUSTUS' SISTER OCTAVIA AND MARK ANTONY

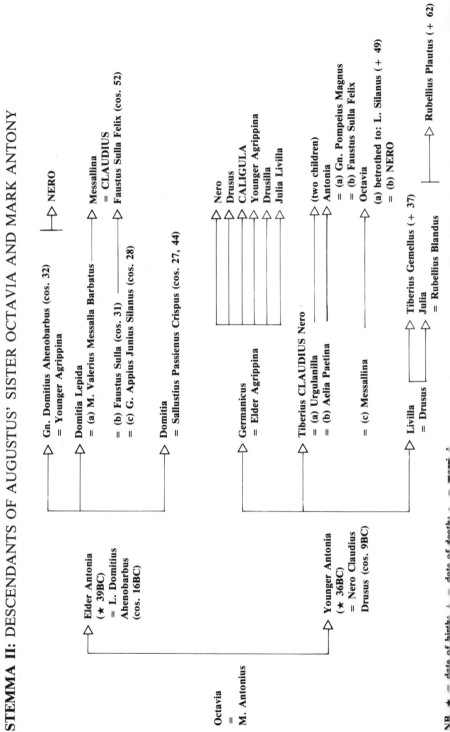

STEMMA III: THE FAMILY OF MARCUS LICINIUS CRASSUS FRUGI

(NB. Some of these relationships are hypothetical)

M. Crassus
(cos. 70 and 55BC: the triumvir)

M. Crassus = Caecilia Metella

M. Crassus (cos. 30BC)
adopts:

M. Crassus Frugi
(born a Piso Frugi)
(cos. 14BC)

Pompey the Great
(cos. 70, 55 and 52BC: the triumvir)

L. Scribonius Libo

L. Scribonius Libo
(cos. 34BC)

Octavian = (1) Scribonia
(**Augustus**)

Elder Julia

Pompeia

L. Scribonius Libo = Magna
(cos. 15BC)

M. Scribonius Libo Drusus
(ex. 16)

L. Scribonius Libo
(cos. AD16)

M. Licinius Crassus Frugi = Scribonia
(cos. AD27, ex. 47)   (ex. 47)

Licinia = L. Calpurnius Piso
Magna   (cos. 57, ex. 70)

C. Calpurnius Piso (ex. 65)
= (1) Livia Orestilla
= (2) Atria Galla

(daughter) = Calpurnius Piso Galerianus
(ex. 70)

Gn. Pompeius Magnus
(ex. 47)
= **Antonia**
(**Claudius' daughter**)

L. Calpurnius
Piso Frugi Licinianus
(adopted by Galba)

M. Licinius Crassus Frugi
(cos. 64, ex. 67)

Licinius Crassus
Scribonianus

NB: ex. = date of execution; = = married

Others who have been related to Scribonia include:
Scribonius Proculus (ex. AD40) and his sons P. Sulpicius
Scribonius Proculus and Scribonius Rufus (both ex. AD67);
L. Arruntius Camillus Scribonianus (ex. AD42).

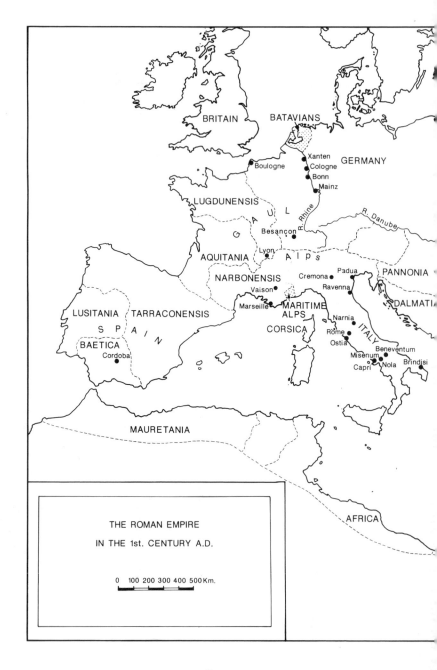

BRITAIN

BATAVIANS

GERMANY

Xanten
Boulogne
Cologne
Bonn
Mainz

LUGDUNENSIS

G A U L

R. Rhine

R. Danube

Besançon

AQUITANIA

Lyon

A l p s

PANNONIA

NARBONENSIS

Cremona

Padua

Vaison

Ravenna

DALMATI

LUSITANIA

TARRACONENSIS

Marseille

MARITIME
ALPS

S P A I N

Narnia

BAETICA

CORSICA

Rome

ITALY

Cordoba

Ostia

Beneventum

Misenum

Nola

Brindisi

Capri

MAURETANIA

THE ROMAN EMPIRE

IN THE 1st. CENTURY A.D.

AFRICA

0   100 200 300 400 500 Km.

xii

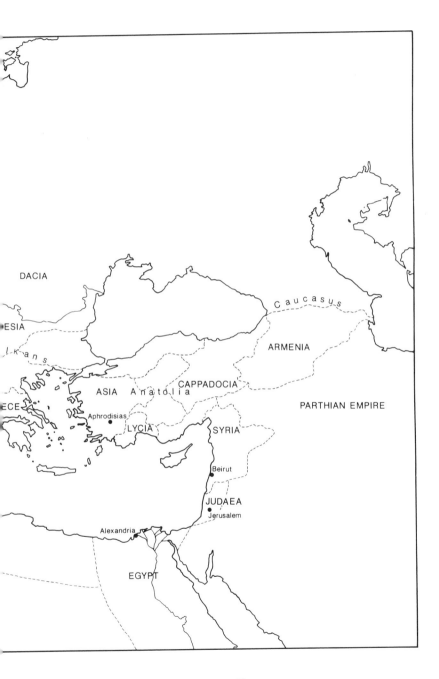

SOURCES AND SUBJECT-MATTER

Chapter 1
Politics under the Principate

In recent years, purely political history has become less fashionable. Why should we study the plottings and killings of a small number of Romans, at best a search for glory won at the expense of the millions of ordinary men and women on whose lives a little light may be thrown by economic and social history? There were other elites – writers, philosophers, artists, even lawyers – whose contributions to the well-being of subsequent generations was more lasting. Of course, the activities of those who have power are often more interesting than those of ordinary people, if only because a much wider range of choices is open to them. And what politicians do affects everyone: in the first place the other politicians with whom they are in immediate contact, but also the ordinary people whom they help and harm through judicial decisions and legislation, and most spectacularly, when consensus breaks down, through wars.

Political history is about power. It is an account of who obtained power (and why), and how they chose to exercise that power. Historians of the principate have pointed out that in every political system, no matter how monarchical, power is in fact exercised by a wide range of persons of different statuses, some in virtue of the office they hold, others because of their wealth or connections or other extra-constitutional factors (as argued by Sir Ronald Syme in *The Roman Revolution*). But we should not overestimate the continuity between the 'republic' and the 'principate'. In the second century BC there was a genuine, if limited, pluralism in the competition for office and power at Rome. After the Social War of 90-88 BC, the Romans extended the right to participate in politics as full citizens to the whole of Italy south of the Apennines. The loyalty of these new citizens (that is to say, the few hundred of them who wanted to become magistrates and senators at Rome, and were wealthy enough) was harnessed by a very small number of families who had the means to do so – notably those of Pompey, Crassus, Antony, and Caesar. Cassius Dio calls Rome's constitution during the following fifty years no longer a republic, but not yet a monarchy, 'the rule of a few dynasts' (*dynasteia*); we might say that it was a political oligopoly. When Octavian defeated Mark Antony at the Battle of Actium in 31 BC, he concentrated the ultimate authority to take all decisions into his own hands. Of course individual magistrates and officials continued to take decisions on the spot; but they were now answerable to one man. It was no longer possible, for example, for a provincial governor to wage war against the wishes of Augustus.

The fact that Augustus claimed to have restored the republican constitution, that the republican magistrates such as consuls, praetors, quaestors and aediles continued to be elected and exercise the functions of their office, and that the emperor himself received his power to exercise command (*imperium*) by virtue of a law passed by the people, shows that formal constitutions do not always reflect the realities of the political system. The descendants of political figures who had been powerful in the republic continued to compete for political office. But the award of prizes by the people at election time increasingly became just a matter of form. Under Augustus, 'important elections were decided by the emperor, but some were left to the electoral units' (Tacitus, *Annals* I, 15.1). Those who were chosen could now exercise only as much power as the emperor allowed. When we find men with names such as Pompeius Magnus, Crassus, Cassius, Aemilius Lepidus or Piso holding the consular office or leading armies as legates of Caesar, that was not because they inherited wealth and influence from their republican ancestors (as many of them certainly did), but because the emperor decided that it was in his interest to make use of their support. If that support was no longer needed, or the emperor feared that he might lose control of the way a man was exercising his power, he disappeared from political life.

The concentration of authority in the hands of one man means that we cannot understand the politics of the principate by reference to formal constitutional rules and procedures. Even under the republic, such rules had played a very much smaller role in defining Roman behaviour than did precedents (*exempla*) or custom (*mos maiorum*). But politics had been 'open': where power was shared between a group of men, they had to justify their proposals and decisions in public. The emperor made up his own mind, though like other Romans he was obliged to listen to the advice of the friends he invited to participate in his *consilium*. If he was acting as a magistrate, the Senate was his *consilium*, and statements made before the Senate were published (Tacitus makes much use of these *Acta Senatus*). But many important political decisions were taken after discussion in the emperor's household *consilium*; and, as Cassius Dio points out (53,19), this meant that the reasons for particular decisions were often never made public, and speculation and rumour took the place of fact as they had not done when politics was 'open' under the republic.

Political life was in fact no longer centred on the Senate or the popular assemblies, but on the Household of Caesar, the *domus Caesaris*. Consequently we cannot understand the politics of the period without taking into account certain Roman social institutions which at first sight have nothing to do with formal politics – for example, the way in which wealthy Romans could use the institution of slavery to enable them to do things by means of their slaves and freedmen which no free-born citizen would have been prepared to do for them. One mundane, but crucial, service was carrying messages. The Romans had developed no state-controlled postal system to help them govern their empire. Arranging for the transmission of messages to and from the provinces was left to individual governors, or the associations of traders and tax collectors. Because the *domus Caesaris* owned estates spread throughout the empire, the Caesars had members of their household in every province, and needed to know what was going on. As a result, they were better informed about events outside Rome than any other politician could be. And they had representatives, 'procurators', on the spot to exercise control on their behalf (often including keeping a check on the provincial governors). These representatives often belonged to provincial families which had been granted Roman citizenship because of their loyalty to past Caesars (e.g. Julius Classicianus in Britain: Tacitus, *Annals* XIV, 38f.). But procurators were not constitutional officials of the Roman state: they were part of the *domus Caesaris*, and their loyalty was to the head of that family.

The head of a Roman household, *paterfamilias*, had the obligation to protect the free and slave members of that household. He also had to support the friends, *amici*, of his family, for example in litigation or at election time. Caesar helped his friends by arbitrating in disputes between them, or recommending them to the people for election. This exercise of favour might be arbitrary. The client kings whom the Romans allowed to rule parts of the Mediterranean world (especially in the east) might be deposed without notice, for they owed their thrones to no legal right, but to the fact that they were a particular Caesar's friends. It is not always appropriate to search for long term 'policies' in the way emperors like Caligula behaved towards these kings. Indeed, 'policymaking' in the modern sense played no significant role in the ancient world. When an emperor founded a new colony, or gave provincials the rights of Roman citizens or remitted taxes, he was not primarily pursuing conscious policies of Romanisation or financial or economic improvement, but exercising his power to do good to his friends and clients.

Patronage or favour (*gratia*) was a social fact, not a constitutional right. But its political significance was enormous. It meant that everyone who had been elected to a magistracy, or held any place in public life at all, owed gratitude to Caesar. Caesar was their 'father', at least as regards their public existence; hence the emperors were acclaimed as *pater patriae*, 'father of the community' (only Tiberius refused the title). The implication was that anyone who offended Caesar had to abandon public life. *Amicitia* was a formal thing, and might be formally revoked. If the friendship of Caesar was revoked, the logical response was to go into exile or commit suicide.

Loyalty to a *paterfamilias* included loyalty to his family; we can see this from the wording of the oaths that communities throughout the empire took to a new emperor, such as Caligula (Braund 562 = Sherk 41). Loyalty to a Caesar, like loyalty to any other *paterfamilias*, passed to his heirs. This explains how the office of emperor could at one and the same time be elective (*imperium* being granted by the sovereign people, on a recommendation of the Senate) and hereditary. The man who inherited the 'household of Caesar' from his predecessor not only controlled what was by far the wealthiest and most powerful household in Rome; he had also inherited the political loyalty of every senator, since every senator owed gratitude to his predecessor.

In one sense, this made it easy for political power to be transferred from one man to another. There was no need for electoral conflict, or party intrigue, or recourse to violence (except where the system broke down in AD 69). On the other hand it subjected the succession to the normal Roman law of inheritance; and Roman law recognised the claims of a wide range of family members. When a *paterfamilias* died without having made a will, his property was divided equally among all those who had been under his *potestas* (legal control): his widow (if she had been *in manu*), his sons, and his daughters. Adopted children (e.g., Tiberius by Augustus) had the same rights as natural children. If these heirs failed, brothers and sisters, and then uncles and aunts, and their descendants, could stake a claim. Throughout the Julio-Claudian period, there were consequently many Romans who, if the current emperor had no direct heir, might be considered to have some claim to head the *domus Caesaris* because they were related to Augustus (Stemma I), to his sister Octavia (Stemma II), or to his first wife Scribonia (Stemma III). The situation was made even more complicated by the tendency for rich Romans to practise divorce and re-marriage (what anthropologists call 'serial monogamy'). Neither family names, nor the accounts of historians such as Tacitus, make it clear that men and women with names like Agrippina and Messallina, Faustus Sulla Felix, Domitius Ahenobarbus and Junius Silanus, were all descendants of Augustus or his sister.

One significant feature of Roman inheritance law was the absence of primogeniture (the principle that all property passes to the eldest son, developed in north-western Europe in the tenth century AD when expensive castle-building began). Another was the principle that females had a claim on the estate, something not usual in agrarian societies. Women could not of course become emperor, because they could hold no public office; but they had claims on a deceased emperor's property, both on their own behalf, and on that of their children. If such children were under age, their fathers (and even step-fathers) might regard it as legitimate to act to protect their interests. This implied that the succession was open to yet another category of claimants, the husbands of imperial princesses.

This explains why the question of who the emperor allowed to marry his daughters (or granddaughters) was so important. After the death of his nephew Marcellus, Augustus gave his daughter Julia to his chosen successor: first to Agrippa, then to Tiberius. A sexual liaison between a princess and a powerful politician was not just a moral delict (punished by exile to an island), it was a political threat. Thus Augustus' daughter Julia was exiled in 2 BC for having an affair with Mark Antony's son Iullus Antonius and/or other aristocrats. These men in fact wanted to ensure that if Augustus died, they would control the *domus Caesaris* through Julia (Julia's husband Tiberius was living in disgrace at Rhodes at the time). Almost the same thing happened in AD 8, when Augustus' granddaughter Julia the Younger was exiled for similar reasons. What lay behind this was an attempt by her husband, Lucius Aemilius Paullus, to oust Tiberius from the succession. Throughout this period, emperors had to be wary of the husbands of women descended from Augustus.

Although it would be extreme to say that 'policies' played no role at all in 'politics' under the Julio-Claudians, it is no exaggeration to say that the most important policy every emperor had was to control his own succession: to decide, not just who would be his heir, but when. That meant keeping his options open for as long as possible, because an heir-apparent less loyal to the incumbent than Tiberius was to Augustus might well be tempted to commit murder in order to speed his accession. Most of the 'political' actions undertaken by an emperor, including the exercise of the massive military force which his control of the Roman army provided him with, were undertaken primarily with the aim of retaining power, and retaining the power to control the succession. Roman emperors should not be credited with wide-ranging strategic defensive or offensive policies (certainly after Augustus). As with contemporary politicians, where emperors emphasised their role as military leaders, it was to buttress political weakness (e.g. Claudius' invasion of Britain, or the stress on military glory in Nero's last years).

Chapter 2
Tacitus

Since the fourth century BC, military ability had held pride of place amongst the Roman virtues, and even a peace-loving emperor like Nero had to suggest to his people that warfare was much more important to him than it actually was. This emphasis on warfare in our sources is reinforced by the fact that for the Greeks and Romans, historical writing was a form of literature which, in Herodotus' words, dealt with the same 'great and glorious deeds' as did epics like Homer's *Iliad* or Vergil's *Aeneid* – namely, fighting. There was plenty of such material for Tacitus' account of the period between 69 and 96 AD, the *Histories*, of which only the first four books and part of the fifth (up to AD 70) survive. It is by far the fullest account of the events of AD 69 and 70, and any historical reconstruction of the civil war has to be based on it. But it has its limitations. One is that the emphasis on fighting means that Tacitus describes the two battles of Cremona in great detail, rhetorically amplified, while there is little or no discussion of the political intentions of men like Vitellius, or the strategic plans of Mucianus and Vespasian (even where it might have been possible for Tacitus to discover these). Scholars have sometimes forgotten that the men who appear in Tacitus are characters in a highly dramatic work of literature, and that the rhetorical common-places in their speeches should not be confused with the actual political intentions of historical figures (cf. Galba's remarks when he adopts Piso, *Histories* I, 15 f.).

A further problem is that, while not uncritical of the Flavian dynasty whose protégé he himself was, Tacitus had to use sources which suppressed anything that showed Vespasian up as less than divine. There is not much to indicate the extent of Mucianus' executions of members of the Piso family in AD 70. Nor is it made clear to what extent Antonius Primus' war against Vitellius was actually fought out of loyalty to Galba rather than to Vespasian; and the rebellion of Civilis in the Rhineland, originally in support of Vespasian, is described throughout as though it had been a barbarian uprising against Rome.

9

These problems become much more complicated with Tacitus' later work, known to us as the *Annals*. The surviving books cover the periods AD 14-29 (Books I-V, 5), 31-37 (VI), and 47-66 (XI-XVI). If 'great and glorious deeds' were supposed to be the subject-matter of history, then Tacitus here provides us with an anti-history (much as Lucan's *Pharsalia* is an anti-epic). From the beginning, Tacitus creates a tension between an idealised Roman history as Livy had written it, consisting largely of victories over Rome's external enemies, and his own catalogue of treason accusations, plots and executions. Instead of entering Rome in a triumphal procession like the generals of old, Tiberius leaves Rome for Capri to triumph over victims from his own family. Instead of being great conquerors, Claudius is a fool ruled by his wives and ex-slaves, and Nero performs on the stage; they cannot permit generals like Corbulo to win real wars.

Tacitus adds to this tension by using features of Livian history such as grouping the material by consular years (hence the title *Annals*), ending with religious material and the obituaries of great men. This gives the impression that, at least at the beginning of this period, there were still 'some vestiges of republican pluralism'. This is reinforced by hints that there were potential alternative leaders to Tiberius available on Augustus' death in AD 14: not just Germanicus, but those allegedly described by Augustus as *capaces imperii*, capable of holding power (*Annals* I, 13). Their names are variously given as Marcus Lepidus (cos. AD 6: not Manius Lepidus, cos. AD 11), Asinius Gallus (son of Asinius Pollio, the consul of 40 BC to whom Vergil dedicated the Fourth Eclogue), Lucius Arruntius, and Gnaeus Piso. If Tacitus believed that these men might have governed instead of the House of Caesar, he was wrong; but two of them were the fathers of later conspirators (Lepidus in 39, Scribonianus in 42). What Tacitus hardly hints at is that most of the alleged conspirators of this period did not seek to replace the 'Caesars', but had some claim to be 'Caesar' themselves, through descent or marriage. By giving little information about such family relationships, Tacitus makes it seem as though the Julio-Claudian emperors' prime concern was to destroy what was left of the republican aristocracy. Tacitus is trying to suggest that the principate became more and more monarchical between AD 14 and 68. This was not so: the monarchy was already absolute under Augustus, who towards the end of his reign executed and exiled conspirators as decisively as any of his successors. Tacitus wanted to avoid saying that, and hence had to begin the *Annals* in AD 14.

Despite his assertion that the *Annals* was written without fear or favour (*sine ira et studio*), his account is coloured by contemporary concerns. One was the intervention of the army in politics; Trajan became emperor because the army had blackmailed Nerva to adopt him in AD 97 (cf. Tacitus' account of Vitellius' coup, or the account of the mutinies in AD 14). Another was the role of 'informers', *delatores*, upwardly mobile senators who accused others of treason against the emperor (see ch. 6); these had been a feature of Domitian's reign. But Tacitus was perhaps less concerned about Domitian's treatment of the Senate (after all, Domitian had appointed Tacitus to several high offices) than Hadrian's. The politics of Hadrian's reign, in so far as they can be reconstructed, were murky: considerable numbers of senators were executed.

There were of course other narrative histories of this period apart from Tacitus'. In the early third century AD, Cassius Dio, a Greek-speaker from Bithynia who became a Roman governor and consul, wrote a history of Rome down to his own time. While his account of the reign of Augustus survived, only excerpts and epitomes compiled by Byzantine scholars exist for the rest of the first century AD. Tacitus' is the only full-scale narrative of this period of which considerable portions survive, and thus has to provide the framework for our other evidence.

Chapter 3
Other Literary and Archaeological Sources

Tacitus and Cassius Dio provide us with a narrative framework for the history of this period. Other sources may be considered together, for – broadly speaking – they do not give us a coherent account of events, but rather provide us with anecdotes and information about particular events which only become significant when we put them into the context of our general picture of the period. Indeed some epigraphical sources (lists of consuls and official calendars, the *Fasti*, or the minutes of meetings of the 'Arval Brethren') contribute more to the overall framework than literary accounts, e.g. for the reign of Caligula, where Tacitus is lost, and Suetonius' *Life* (written in the reign of Hadrian) gives us a series of anecdotes rather than a biography in the modern sense.

The Latin *vita*, 'life', does not indicate a sequence of events in chronological order, but a description of a person's character or lifestyle. Hence there are considerable problems about using Suetonius as a historical source: he is often completely uninterested in telling us the exact circumstances of a particular event (e.g. when did Tiberius reject Claudius' 'legitimate demands for political office' (Suetonius, *Claudius* 5): was it before or after the death of Germanicus?). This lack of context reinforces the impression that emperors did the most extraordinary things for no apparent reason. This is particularly so in the case of those emperors classified as 'bad' because they had alienated the senators whose collective memory by and large created the historical tradition. Considerable sections of the *Lives* of Tiberius, Caligula, and Nero consist of lists of more or less scandalous anecdotes, some invented, but most based on facts of which we do not have the context. Suetonius was simply taking the rhetorician's framework of what an invective (speech criticising an opponent) ought to contain, and applying it to these emperors. Not surprisingly, we find many of the *topoi* (literary commonplaces) associated in Greek rhetoric with typical tyrants (the tyrant confiscates the property of innocent men to pay for his own extravagance, he kicks his pregnant wife to death, etc.). Many of Plutarch's *Lives*, written in

Greek towards the end of the first century, are similar in approach and format; those of Galba and Otho are very unusual, since the bulk of each of them is a narrative account of the emperor's reign, based on a (lost) Flavian historical source. Where we can compare Plutarch with surviving passages of Tacitus or Dio, the approach is so similar that we may assume that Plutarch faithfully translated his source. Another lost Latin history was used by Josephus, a Jewish supporter of the Flavians, in his account of the assassination of Caligula in the *Ancient History of the Jews* (or *Antiquities*: cf. ch. 9).

Literary texts are historical documents in their own right. Just as Tacitus' account of Civilis' rebellion throws light on the Flavian need to win the loyalty of the Rhine legions, so the short history of Rome written by Velleius Paterculus and dedicated to Marcus Vinicius in AD 30 gives us an insight into the political atmosphere at Rome when Sejanus was at the height of his power (though there is still no consensus among historians as to whether Velleius genuinely approved of Sejanus, feared him, or despised him as an upstart). Another contemporary who refers to the wickedness of Sejanus is Phaedrus in his collection of fables (Prologue to Bk. III, l.41).

Poems and prose essays also contain political statements, and were sometimes composed primarily as propaganda (in the sense of praising or criticising particular people). Seneca's *Apocolocyntosis* ('The Transformation of Claudius into a Pumpkin') is the most overt, and has contributed to the picture of Claudius as a fool who was ruled by his wives and freedmen, but who was also responsible for the execution of many innocent men whom he feared. It was probably written for Nero's enjoyment at the Saturnalia (New Year/Yuletide festival) in AD 54. A similarly hostile view of Claudius is taken in some of the poems of Calpurnius Siculus, also composed under Nero. Under the Flavians, of course, poets attacked Nero in his turn, e.g. in the tragedy *Octavia*, ascribed to Seneca.

Seneca's genuine philosophical writings contain a wealth of anecdotes and examples from recent history. What is missing for this period is anything comparable to the collections of letters which survive for the 50s and 40s BC (Cicero) and the first decade of the second century AD (Pliny). Nor do published speeches throw light on political history in the way Cicero's do for the end of the republic. Philo's attack on a Prefect of Egypt at the beginning of Caligula's reign, the *In Flaccum*, is an exception.

Fig. 1. Lucius Annaeus Seneca (4 BC – AD 65), whose writings have contributed to the negative image of Tiberius, Caligula and Claudius.

A few passages from speeches by Roman emperors survive on Egyptian papyri or were recorded on inscriptions: Claudius' speech to the Senate justifying his inclusion of men of Celtic origin among its numbers is a famous example (Braund 570). It was set up at Lyon, the ceremonial centre of the three Gallic provinces, no doubt by the grateful senators concerned. Some other important historical documents have survived on stone or bronze, for instance the law granting Vespasian imperial power (see ch. 18). Particularly interesting are the minutes of meetings of a religious fraternity called the 'Arval Brethren', who in this period consisted of important political figures who met to sacrifice for the welfare of the emperor and his household. These minutes give us the dates on which births and deaths occurred, as well as the detection of conspiracies (e.g. under Caligula). Sometimes we can even make deductions about which members of the fraternity were absent from Rome, e.g. during the fighting of 69 AD. The original Latin or Greek texts of most of these documents are usefully assembled in the collections by Ehrenberg & Jones, Smallwood, and McCrum & Woodhead; many are translated in the selections by Braund and Sherk (see *Further Reading*).

The view held by the great nineteenth century historians Ranke and Mommsen, that documents were more reliable or truthful than literary sources, is no longer accepted. Roman coins may exemplify how 'documents' need interpretation just as much (though in different ways) as a literary text. The images on a coin have to be deciphered, and the legend translated. The same image means different things in different contexts. In AD 66, Nero struck coins depicting Jupiter the Liberator to advertise the freeing of Greece from the direct rule of a Roman governor; in AD 68, Vindex minted coins with an identical image when he threw off his allegiance to Nero. To understand the force of the propaganda contained in the message, we need to know just who decided on the legend, and who was intended to read it (e.g. were the coins advertising the praetorian guard's loyalty to Claudius intended to be seen only by them, as part of the donative promised in AD 41, or were they intended for a wider audience, perhaps as a snub to the Senate? For whose eyes were the inscriptions on Vindex's and Classicus' coins in AD 68-70 intended?). Furthermore, some coins were clearly struck by people who were out of touch with affairs at Rome, e.g. coins minted at Lyon representing Tiberius as a god.

Epigraphy – the study of inscriptions on stone or metal, especially tombstones – can tell us a great deal about the careers of wealthy Roman officials who otherwise left few traces in the literary record. Epigraphers have developed a specialist discipline called prosopography, tracing the careers and family relationships of individual Romans. Prosopography has its limitations – it cannot take account of factors which are not recorded on inscriptions, such as the patronage or particular skills which allowed an individual to reach high office; but it has been an immeasurable help in establishing exactly how powerful figures mentioned by Tacitus and others were related, and distinguishing between different individuals who shared common names (especially females, since Roman women were formally only called by their family name, e.g. Junia or Domitia).

Archaeology, too, can help to fill in the framework provided by literary sources. In recent years, archaeologists have found the grotto at Sperlonga patronised by Tiberius for his picnics, where Sejanus saved his life when the roof collapsed (see ch. 6); or the patrician palaces destroyed in the great fire of AD 64, confiscated by Nero for his 'Golden House'. Statues and reliefs show us how Roman emperors wanted to be seen by their people, and what it was about their rulers that provincials thought deserved respect (e.g. the conquest of 'Bretannia' depicted on a shrine to the Julio-Claudians at Aphrodisias in far-away Asia: *Journal of Roman Studies* 77 (1987), plate xiv). But by and large epigraphy and archaeology are of more use to the social or economic historian. For political history, we still have to rely in the first instance on Tacitus.

TIBERIUS

Chapter 4
The Accession

The moment when power is transferred from one person to another is the critical point where the nature and complexity of that power become particularly clear. The recognition that Tiberius was the new emperor when Augustus died on August 19th, AD 14, was one of the least problematic of such 'accessions' in the period under consideration. But that was only because the last, bloody, years of Augustus had seen the elimination of many potential rivals to Tiberius, especially in the aftermath of the conspiracies involving his daughter and granddaughter in 2 BC and AD 8. Nevertheless there was no precedent for the peaceful recognition of a single man as ruler of Rome: Sulla, Julius Caesar and Octavian had all been accepted as such as a matter of necessity, the result of the outcome of civil war.

We have seen (ch. 1) that before anything else, the Roman Senate and people accepted the control of their affairs by a particular individual because he was 'Caesar', the head of the *domus Caesaris*. Roman law allowed a rich *paterfamilias* the right to leave most of his property as he pleased in his will; but it also recognised the claims of all those who had been under his immediate *potestas* (his widow and those of his sons and daughters, whether natural or adopted, who were still *in potestate*) to equal shares in the inheritance. These two principles could sometimes conflict (and the law allowed those who felt that they had been unjustly ignored in a will to appeal against it, the *querella inofficiosi testamenti*). Since succession to the household of Caesar was in accordance with the same rules as applied to any other household, the same potential for conflict and complaint existed. Augustus made it clear in his will, read out to the Senate even before his funeral, that Tiberius was to be his successor (his widow Livia, as a woman, was excluded from formal political life, though she inherited one third of the estate); Augustus explained that he had adopted Tiberius because his two natural grandchildren, Gaius and Lucius, had died. (That was not a slight on Tiberius, but a public justification of the adoption.) There was no mention of Agrippa Postumus, the grandson whom Augustus had formally adopted in AD

4, at the same time as he adopted Tiberius. In AD 8 or 9, in virtue of his *patriapotestas*, Augustus banished him to the island of Planasia; but there is no evidence that the adoption had been rescinded. Under Roman law, a son could only be disinherited in a will if he was explicitly named: so it was just conceivable that opponents of Tiberius might put forward the claims of Postumus. Postumus had to be killed – in Tacitus' words, the first charge to be made against the new reign, though it was not clear whether the execution had already been arranged by Augustus. It was an embarrassment to Tiberius, and a promised investigation into who carried out the killing was never allowed to proceed.

Tiberius' claim to be Augustus' sole legitimate successor was entirely valid, but that was not enough. He also had to be in actual control of the household. Roman law had developed a theory of ownership which, for most practical purposes, granted the man who had control (*possessio*) of an estate full legal recognition until such time as someone else had proved that he had a better claim before a court of law – hence the phrase, 'possession is nine parts of the law'. Since the man with *possessio* over the household of Caesar was also the ruler of Rome, no court was likely to rule against him, however legitimate the claims of his rival. It was essential that Tiberius should take *possessio* the moment that Augustus died; hence Livia's urgency in summoning him to Nola to be at Augustus' bedside, and hence also the unfounded rumours, duly reported by Tacitus, that Livia held back news of Augustus' death until Tiberius had arrived, or alternatively even hastened his death in order to make sure that Tiberius should not be too far away (similar rumours circulated about Hadrian's accession in AD 117).

The question of the succession was solved the moment Tiberius had *possessio* of the household of Caesar. The first thing he did as the new Caesar was to write to inform all Roman armies of the fact (Cassius Dio 57, 2.1). Those individuals in public life who considered themselves to be clients of the *domus Caesaris* immediately took a personal oath of loyalty to Tiberius as the new Caesar: first the consuls, prefects, senators and people at Rome, and later individuals and communities throughout the empire. All that the Senate had to do was recognise the fact of his power; that this fact was legitimate was made manifest when Tiberius had Augustus' will read out. In AD 14, the Senate did not even have to recommend that the people grant the new emperor *imperium*, the formal military and civil powers of the supreme Roman magistrate, for Tiberius had already held these powers as Augustus' colleague since AD 12. Tacitus misleadingly suggests that the Senate had some freedom of action in AD 14. He emphasises that on his return to Rome with Augustus' body, Tiberius summoned a meeting of the Senate to make arrangements for the funeral in virtue not of *imperium*, but of *tribunicia potestas*; and he describes in some detail a meeting on September 17th at which Tiberius is said to have wondered whether to accept the imperial office at all, in order to force other potential emperors to show their hand. Tacitus accepts that Augustus had listed three such possible candidates, men who were *capax imperii* (see ch. 2). As a result, he leaves the reader with the entirely false impression that someone other than Tiberius might have held, or shared, Augustus' powers. There was no question of that. What the Senate actually debated on September 17th was how wide Tiberius' responsibilities (*cura*) ought to be – whether Tiberius should have the duty to oversee all those areas of public life that Augustus had been responsible for.

Not only does Tacitus give an impression of much greater fluidity at Rome in AD 14 than was actually the case, he also goes on to describe mutinies amongst the legions in Pannonia and Germany as though they constituted a serious threat to Tiberius' accession. Tacitus himself had experienced the events of AD 97, when a threatened coup by the Rhine army had forced the emperor Nerva to adopt Trajan, and he had written about the Rhine army's attempt to put Vitellius on the throne in AD 69 in his *Histories*; but there was no question in AD 14 of successful military opposition to Tiberius, least of all by proclaiming his adopted son Germanicus (in command of the Rhine army) as emperor. What both groups of legionaries wanted was an improvement in pay and conditions. Tacitus' account makes it clear that many of these soldiers were not volunteers, but men conscripted in the aftermath of the Varus disaster in AD 9. Roman legionaries took their military oath to a particular *imperator* (commander), rather than to the state; the death of Augustus would have required a new oath to a new *imperator*, and might be seen as one of the few occasions on which soldiers could express their grievances from a position of strength. If they were protesting, it was against the way they had been treated during the last years of Augustus, not against the accession of Tiberius. Tiberius sent his son Drusus to deal with the Pannonian mutiny by offering an improvement in pay (though the offer was later rescinded, on the grounds that the military treasury could not find the money). On the Rhine, Germanicus' initial attempts to restore discipline were thwarted by the arrival of a delegation of senior senators from Rome; the soldiers rightly assumed that Tiberius would appeal to the authority of the Senate to deny them the concessions they had won from Germanicus. In the end the mutiny had to be put down by force.

Chapter 5
Germanicus and Drusus

When Augustus adopted Tiberius as his son and successor in AD 4, after the deaths of his own grandchildren Gaius and Lucius, he had also arranged for Tiberius to adopt as his son Germanicus (15 BC-AD 19), the son of Tiberius' brother Drusus and of Augustus' own niece the younger Antonia (Stemma II). Germanicus' wife was Augustus' granddaughter Agrippina; their six children were great-grand-children of both Augustus and Livia (Stemma I). All would have a claim to inherit the House of Caesar after Tiberius.

Tacitus describes the events of the following years as though they were primarily a conflict between the wicked Tiberius and the noble Germanicus. The reason is literary as much as political. Tacitus portrays Tiberius as the opposite of everything that an emperor ought to be; and since Germanicus died before he could become emperor, there were no inconvenient facts to refute the picture of him as (potentially) an ideal ruler. A positive literary source – the memoirs of his daughter, the younger Agrippina – will have helped to create the picture of Germanicus as a new Alexander.

Hence Tacitus glorifies the series of campaigns which Germanicus led into northern Germany in the autumn of AD 14 and the two following summers. These campaigns were costly in resources and casualties, and resulted in no expansion of the territory under Roman control. They were fought largely to re-establish Roman military prestige after the Varus disaster, and to enhance Germanicus' own prestige as a general. It is unlikely that the reason why Tiberius brought these campaigns to an end (appealing to a document written by Augustus which advised against any expansion of the empire) was because he was jealous of Germanicus. Tiberius had achieved quite enough military glory himself during his lifetime. Germanicus' position as Tiberius' successor was sealed by a full triumph in AD 17, and underlined by a joint consulship held in AD 18. In that year Germanicus set off on a tour of the eastern provinces of the empire. One reason for granting Germanicus the *cura* of the east was to oversee the integration of Cappadocia as a province following

Fig. 2. Tacitus' success in persuading later generations that Germanicus might have been an ideal emperor is exemplified by Rubens' The Glorification of Germanicus.

the death of its king Archelaus. The revenue from the new province, together with the end of the German war, allowed Tiberius to halve the 1% sales tax which supported the military treasury. By appointing Germanicus, Tiberius was also following the precedent set by Augustus, who had sent Agrippa, Tiberius himself, and Gaius Caesar to rule the eastern provinces when these men were the heirs-apparent.

As Germanicus' principal adviser, Tiberius appointed a senior consular and personal friend, Gnaeus Calpurnius Piso (cos. 7 BC), to be legate of Syria. We need not believe Tacitus' insinuation that Piso was appointed in order to keep a check on Germanicus; it was rather so that he would have an experienced adviser. Unfortunately Germanicus and Piso quarrelled. Tacitus suggests that this was the result of rivalry between their wives; but an anecdote told by Seneca shows that Piso was noted for his violent temper. When Germanicus exceeded his brief by travelling to Egypt (theoretically out of bounds to any Roman senator), Piso misinterpreted Tiberius' expression of displeasure as a signal that Germanicus had fallen from favour. Germanicus, on his return from Egypt, formally renounced the friendship (*amicitia*) between Piso and the family of the Caesars. Piso had no choice but to abandon his province, but then made the mistake of trying to return by force when he heard that Germanicus had fallen ill. This was illegal, and Piso was prosecuted for treason on his return to Rome. Following Germanicus' death on October 10th AD 19, his

Fig. 3. Brass sestertius, AD 23 (Rome). Two cornucopiae with the heads of Tiberius Gemellus and his twin brother.

widow Agrippina also accused Piso of having poisoned him; there was no evidence to substantiate that charge. In view of what had happened, though, Tiberius could not treat Piso as an *amicus*, and he committed suicide.

The death of Germanicus made Tiberius' own son Drusus the likely successor. He returned from the governorship of Illyricum to celebrate a triumph on May 28th, AD 20. In 21, he shared Tiberius' fourth consulship with him; and his claim was strengthened by the birth of twin sons, celebrated on coins in 22/23. These boys – only one of whom, Tiberius Gemellus ('the twin'), was to survive – were related to Augustus through their mother Livilla and grandmother Antonia the Younger, Augustus' niece. But Drusus died in the following year. Tiberius Gemellus was a baby, and the eldest two sons of Germanicus, Nero and Drusus, had only just received the adult toga; so the question of who might succeed Tiberius as the 'protector' of these young Caesars was wide open.

Fig. 4. Brass dupondius, between AD 21 and 37. On the obverse, 'Tiberius Caesar Augustus, son of the deified Augustus, with eight imperial acclamations'; the reverse represents a ceremonial shield celebrating the emperor's clemency.

There were others who might claim a share in the succession to the Caesars. After Germanicus' death, his brother Claudius might have become the protector of his nephews; but he was firmly prevented from playing a political role by Tiberius and Livia. Claudius survived the rest of Tiberius' reign by pretending to be interested only in scholarship. In September AD 16, Marcus Scribonius Libo had been accused of treason and had committed suicide. Not only was he a great-grandson of Pompey the Great, but his great-aunt Scribonia had been Augustus' wife and the mother of the elder Julia. Tacitus describes this case as though it had been the first of a long series of treason trials throughout Tiberius' reign for which he blames the emperor himself. But Tacitus' own account shows that accusations of *maiestas* by so-called informers should be distinguished from the deadly rivalry for the succession among Augustus' relatives. Towards those not involved in that struggle, Tiberius was willing to exercise clemency – a point that he emphasised on coins struck to advertise the imperial virtues. Thus Decimus Silanus, whose brother Marcus (cos. AD 15) was a close friend of Tiberius, was permitted to return from the exile into which Augustus had sent him in AD 8.

Chapter 6
Sejanus and the Power-Vacuum

The detection of Sejanus' 'conspiracy' on October 18th, AD 31, was one of the most carefully stage-managed events in Roman history. It was commemorated on inscriptions set up throughout Italy, and is mentioned in poetry both contemporary (Phaedrus) and later (Juvenal). Accounts of Tiberius' reign are coloured by the myth that every act of Sejanus' was aimed at seizing the imperial office – for instance, the sensible decision to concentrate the praetorian guard in a single camp on the eastern side of Rome. He was blamed not just for persecuting potential successors to Tiberius, but for a whole number of suicides and deaths – including that of Drusus in AD 23.

Sejanus certainly suggested that Drusus' widow Livilla should marry him. This would have given him unprecedented status – like previous Praetorian Prefects, he was hitherto only an equestrian; and it would have meant that, as Tiberius Gemellus' step-father, Sejanus would be likely to govern the empire until he came of age. But by making that suggestion, he had Tiberius' interest at heart as well as his own. If Tiberius died now, the household of Caesar would pass to Germanicus' widow the elder Agrippina and one of her sons Nero and Drusus – or perhaps to whoever would be Agrippina's husband. In that case, neither Livilla nor her son would long survive.

Agrippina asked Tiberius to provide her with a new husband. She may have had in mind Asinius Gallus, one of the men Augustus had described as *capax imperii*; Tiberius loathed him because he had married Vipsania, the beloved wife Tiberius had been forced to divorce in order to marry Julia (that marriage had also made Gallus the step-father of his son Drusus). Tiberius could not countenance such a liaison for Agrippina. Nor did he like the idea of allowing Livilla to re-marry. The husband of either of these ladies would be in a position to replace Tiberius himself.

In AD 26, Tiberius was 67, an age at which a Roman senator might expect to be allowed to retire. Tiberius had frequently absented himself from Rome before, particularly during the unhealthy summer months; but he now left for the island of Capri, which was to remain his base for the rest of his life. There may be a basis to Tacitus' perverse suggestion that Tiberius left Rome for Capri in order to escape from Livia: although Livia was Tiberius' mother and Gemellus' great-grandmother, she was also the great-grandmother of Agrippina's children, and unlike Tiberius wanted to see one of them as emperor, in accordance with Augustus' wishes. In the course of the journey to Capri, Sejanus bravely saved Tiberius' life when the roof of a cave in which he was picnicking collapsed. Sejanus was well aware that his own survival depended on that of Tiberius. In AD 29, shortly after Livia's death, he had Agrippina and her eldest son Nero arrested for plotting Tiberius' death; at the very least, they will have been making plans against that eventuality. Drusus, Nero's brother and rival, was later also imprisoned. There was no trial, and the three remained in captivity until their deaths.

When Livia died at the age of 86 in AD 29, the funeral oration was given by the third of Germanicus' sons, Gaius Caligula (born August 31st, AD 12). Tiberius did not bother to return to Rome for the occasion. Caligula was formally still a child; after Livia's death he lived in the household of the younger Antonia, who protected him for the next three years, until she persuaded Tiberius to let him play a role in public life.

One remarkable feature of Livia's will was that she bestowed an enormous legacy of fifty million sesterces on a thirty-year-old patrician called Servius Sulpicius Galba (born 3 BC). Galba was the step-son of Livia Ocellina, a close relative of Livia's. Tiberius rightly interpreted this legacy as a personal insult, and revised it downwards by a factor of one hundred. But it was a sign that Galba was more than just an ordinary patrician. During his praetorship, he had put on a show of tightrope-walking elephants. Tiberius was said to have worked out his horoscope and pronounced that Galba was destined to be emperor one day.

Tiberius' absence from Rome during these years had two serious consequences. The first was that he was unable to control proceedings in the Senate. As a result his reign became infamous for a number of treason trials for which he was blamed. In fact these accusations of treason (*maiestas*) were never initiated by him, and rarely of any advantage to him. Ambitious senators initiated these accusations because, in the absence of opportunities to win glory through military campaigns, such trials were the best way of making a name for oneself, eliminating rivals, getting a quarter of the accused's property as a reward, and proving oneself a loyal supporter of the emperor.

The other dangerous consequence of Tiberius' absence from Rome was that it meant that all access to the emperor had to be channelled via Sejanus. Sejanus was a mere equestrian; by the time Velleius Paterculus was writing his *Histories*, his pivotal role had provoked considerable resentment among senators. For Sejanus to have married Livilla would have been going too far (although one very late source, John of Antioch, says that Tiberius actually 'called him his child (i.e. son-in-law) and successor'). And in AD 31 Tiberius held his fifth consulship with Sejanus (although until now not a senator) as his colleague; his previous colleagues had been the heirs-apparent Germanicus and Drusus.

Fig. 5. Brass dupondius, AD 37-8 (Rome). Portrait of the younger Antonia, widow of Tiberius' brother Drusus and a powerful figure during the last years of Tiberius' reign.

It was at this point that the younger Antonia – widow of Tiberius' brother – succeeded in persuading Tiberius that Sejanus' power was not only unacceptable to senators, but constituted a threat to Tiberius himself as well as to Agrippina and her children. Germanicus' remaining son, Gaius Caligula, was transferred to the safety of Tiberius' entourage at Capri. With the assistance of Sutorius Macro, Prefect of the *vigiles* (the urban police force), Tiberius plotted Sejanus' elimination.

No senators had been executed since Tiberius' accession (although several had had to commit suicide). His ruthlessness against Sejanus consequently came as a complete shock. On October 18th, AD 31, a letter from the emperor was read out to the Senate in Sejanus' presence. It was long and difficult to follow (in Juvenal's words, *grandis et verbosa*). It ended by denouncing Sejanus as a traitor. Sejanus had expected the letter to recommend that he be granted *tribunicia potestas* as Tiberius' colleague; instead he found himself stripped of his office (a second letter appointed Macro Praetorian Prefect). He was executed the same day; the *Fasti* record the suicide of his wife Apicata and the execution of his children the following week. Before she died, Apicata accused Livilla of having been Sejanus' associate in the poisoning of Tiberius' son Drusus.

Chapter 7
The Aftermath of Sejanus: a Reign of Terror?

Tiberius ensured that the unmasking of Sejanus' 'conspiracy' would be hailed as an event of great significance. But we should not be misled into believing that it was a political watershed. Tiberius continued to reside at Capri, and accusations of *maiestas* continued to be made by informers against their personal enemies – though now the charges generally included that of 'having been a friend of Sejanus'. But the number of those executed on Tiberius' orders was very small. Even Sejanus' uncle, Junius Blaesus, was not executed but committed suicide after Tiberius had renounced his *amicitia*; and Blaesus' two sons even survived until AD 36.

Although Tacitus maximises the dangers facing the powerful and wealthy at this time, Tiberius' failure to control trials in the Senate brought a number of leading senators to grief. Lucius Arruntius (cos. AD 6) was another of those described as *capax imperii* by Augustus. Nevertheless we should beware of assuming that Tiberius caused his suicide (c. AD 35): his adopted son, L. Arruntius Camillus Scribonianus, held a consulship in AD 32 , and was then allowed to remain in command of the army of Lower Germany until the end of Tiberius' reign. Others accused were Gaius Annius Pollio and his son Lucius Annius Vinicianus. The son at least survived to hold a suffect consulship and to be considered an imperial candidate after Caligula's assassination in 41. Another who survived an accusation of *maiestas* was Gaius Appius Silanus (cos. 28, probably the cousin of Tiberius' friend, the consul of 15). These cases show that treason trials are an indication of the rivalry between families and individuals rather than of a 'reign of terror' brought about by Tiberius' fear of opposition. The evidence suggests that, throughout his reign, Tiberius tried (sometimes ineffectually) to moderate such criminal accusations.

Tiberius' justified fear was that he would be supplanted by someone within his own family. Germanicus' oldest son Nero had already been killed (his death could be blamed on Sejanus); but Tiberius did not release Drusus, who died in 33. Although Caligula was ten years older than Gemellus, Tiberius appears not to have considered him a threat; his astrologer Thrasyllus had promised Tiberius another ten years of life, and perhaps he felt that that would suffice to introduce Gemellus to public life. Caligula was made a member of the college of augurs and a *pontifex*, and in 33 he held the office of quaestor. More importantly, Tiberius tried to tie Caligula closer to him by marrying him to Junia Claudilla, the daughter of his old supporter Marcus Junius Silanus (cos. 15). This meant that Silanus, too, was in a strong position, as the potential guardian of any children the marriage might bring; but in fact Junia died in childbirth in c. 36.

But Tiberius also brought a number of other men into prominence by marrying them to the princesses of the *domus Caesaris*. Both Agrippina and Livilla were too dangerous to be permitted to re-marry, and were left to starve to death in custody, as was Asinius Gallus (AD 33). But Germanicus' daughter Drusilla was married to Lucius Cassius Longinus (cos. ord. 30); his descent from the tyrannicide Cassius should not be allowed to mask the fact that his political importance was derived from his close association with the Caesars. His brother Gaius Cassius Longinus (cos. suff. 30) may already have been the husband of Augustus' great-granddaughter Junia Lepida. Agrippina the Younger was given to L. Domitius Ahenobarbus, son of the elder Antonia (and thus grandnephew of Augustus); it is interesting that they thought it best not to have any children while Tiberius was still alive. In 33, Germanicus' youngest daughter, Julia Livilla (*AD 18), married Marcus Vinicius (the dedicatee of Velleius Paterculus' *Histories*). His grandfather, the consul of 19 BC, had been one of Tiberius' early generals in Illyricum and Germany. Vinicius himself had been consul in 30. In the same year, Tiberius' granddaughter Livia Julia married again. Her husband was Gaius Rubellius Blandus (cos. suff. AD 18), whose grandfather had taught Tiberius rhetoric. Blandus' relative insignificance suggests that Tiberius selected him precisely because he was not likely to be taken seriously as an imperial candidate, and hence was no rival to Gemellus. Nevertheless their son Rubellius Plautus was to be a source of fear to Nero, until he had him killed in 62. These men were allowed to appear in public as close associates of Tiberius. When large areas of Rome were destroyed by fire in 34, Tiberius appointed the four *progeneri Caesaris* ('sons-in-law of Caesar') to supervise the distribution of relief aid on his behalf.

These years also saw the rise to prominence of several other figures who were to play a role in later political events. A number of them were protégés of Antonia. Lucius Vitellius, who was to become Claudius' principal adviser and the father of the later emperor, was *consul ordinarius* in 34, and in 35 a suffect consulship was held by his friend Valerius Asiaticus from Vienne. Flavius Sabinus, City Prefect under Nero, Otho and Vitellius, and the brother of Vespasian, entered the Senate in AD 34 or 35. Galba was *consul ordinarius* in AD 33; his suffect was Lucius Salvius Otho, the father of another emperor.

Although absent from Rome, Tiberius continued to carry out his duties as *princeps*. In AD 34, he arranged relief after the serious fire, and assisted the cities of the province of Asia following damage by an earthquake (as he had already done in 22). He also intervened to avoid a major crisis of credit in 33, apparently caused by a shortage of coin. We should not assume that Roman emperors had any concept of an 'economic policy'; but they did see it as their job to make the wealthy feel secure in the possession of their property. Tiberius' own absence from the courtrooms of Rome was comparatively un-important, though of course it made life much more difficult for litigants (who might have to travel to Capri) and was a major reason for the emperor's steadily increasing unpopularity. The other was that he had no wish to put on any games for the people of Rome, and restricted the opportunities that candidates for office had to provide such games. At the very beginning of his reign he had abolished the requirement for praetors to present themselves for election by the people, thus making it unnecessary for candidates to bribe the electorate with games.

Tiberius died on March 16th, AD 37, at Misenum (Dio dates his death ten days later). He was on his way back to Rome. The following day was the festival of the Liberalia, on which children were traditionally given their adult toga and enrolled as citizens. It is conceivable that Tiberius intended to give his fifteen-year-old grandson Tiberius Gemellus the adult toga on that day. So far he had not done anything to bring Gemellus into the limelight, possibly because of Thrasyllus' assurance that he had ten more years to live. Whether or not Caligula and Macro assisted Tiberius' death by smothering him with a pillow, it left Caligula in *possessio* of the household of Caesar.

CALIGULA, CLAUDIUS AND NERO

Chapter 8
A New Gaius Julius Caesar

With Macro's support, Caligula's accession was reported to the palace and to the praetorians at Rome, and he was acclaimed by the Senate on March 18th, AD 37. Tiberius' will was read out. It instituted Caligula and Tiberius Gemellus as joint heirs. Gemellus was still a child unqualified for office; the Senate had no qualms about setting the will aside (in accordance with Roman law, a reason had to be found: the testator was declared 'insane'). Caligula expressed his intention of adopting Gemellus to make his inferiority manifest, and declared him *princeps iuventutis*, i.e. effectively his successor, to obviate any grounds for complaint on the part of those who upheld the claims of Tiberius' descendants.

Macro and Caligula arrived in Rome on the 28th, and Caligula formally accepted the powers allotted to him by the Senate. Tiberius' funeral on April 3rd followed the lines of Augustus' funeral, and the late emperor's apotheosis was duly reported to the Senate. The mint at Lyon struck gold coins representing Tiberius as a god. The moneyers had jumped the gun: Tiberius was so unpopular with both senators and people that no divine honours were in fact granted.

Caligula emphasised that he intended to show more respect to Senate and people than Tiberius had. Exiles were recalled, and coins minted with the slogan 'For Citizens Saved', OB CIVES SERVATOS. To deal with the backlog of legal business caused by Tiberius' absence from Rome, a fifth panel of jurors was instituted. To please the people, spectacles were organised; and to honour the Senate, Caligula asked formal permission for the privilege of exhibiting more gladiators than permitted by law. Elections were returned to the people – effectively a way of making candidates provide games. The *Fasti* report that on June 1st and on July 19th, 75 sesterces were distributed to each citizen in largesse. The army was not forgotten: Caligula doubled the 500 sesterces left to each soldier in Tiberius' will.

Another reason for Tiberius' unpopularity had been that his reign had seen very little public building activity. Caligula started major work on the palace, including a ramp or bridge to give direct access to the forum. All of this was expensive. The theme that tyrants waste money is a literary commonplace, and it is difficult to believe that within a year Caligula spent the 2.7 billion sesterces (probably the capital value of the imperial household) left by Tiberius. But expenditure will soon have outrun income; the Roman banking system knew nothing corresponding to a National Debt or loans to the Government, and even the wealthiest state finds itself in difficulties if major expenditure has to be met from the income from annual agricultural surpluses.

Caligula represented himself as the centre of a family. Coins showed the head of his mother Agrippina (through whom he was Augustus' great-grandson), his brothers 'The Caesars Nero and Drusus' who had died under Tiberius, and his three sisters Agrippina, Drusilla and Julia (Livilla). The divine honours that had been voted but never instituted were paid to Livia, and, after her death on May 1st, also to Caligula's grandmother Antonia the Younger. His uncle Claudius, snubbed by Tiberius, was chosen to share the consulship with Caligula in July and August.

By representing himself as reversing the attitudes of his predecessor, Caligula necessarily alienated those who had been loyal to him. Naturally, little can be said about them: they may have included Flaccus, the Prefect of Egypt attacked by Philo. Their leader seems to have been Marcus Junius Silanus (cos. 15), whose daughter Tiberius had made Caligula marry. By combining two separate anecdotes found in Suetonius, we may deduce that Silanus used the opportunity of Caligula's sea-journey to bring his mother's ashes back from the island of Planasia (where she had died in exile) for an unsuccessful coup. Both Silanus and Gemellus were put to death (or required to commit suicide).

Ancient writers explained the paradox of Caligula's early promise and later execration as a 'tyrant' as due to a sudden change of character, variously ascribed to escape from the restraints imposed by his grandmother or his sister, to illness, or to the effects of over-indulgence. Such a distinction is invalid. From the start, Caligula did not hesitate to eliminate anyone who threatened him. (He quickly decided to dispense with Macro.) That Caligula represented himself as Hercules (and was so flattered by others, such as Lentulus Gaetulicus, legate of Upper Germany since AD 30) was not a sign of madness, but of a widespread view that a good ruler should defend civilization against barbarism, as Hercules had done. If he did well,

Fig. 6. Brass sestertius, AD 37-8 (Rome). Portrait of the elder Agrippina, 'Agrippina, daughter of Marcus, mother of Gaius Caesar Augustus'.

Fig. 7. Brass sestertius, AD 37-8 (Rome). Caligula's sisters, AGRIPPINA (represented as the goddess of Security), DRUSILLA (as Concord) and IULIA (as Good Fortune).

Fig. 8. Brass dupondius, AD 37-8 (Rome). Caligula's deceased brothers, NERO ET DRUSUS CAESARES.

he would – like Hercules – be rewarded with a place in heaven. During Caligula's reign, the only provincials who raised difficulties about paying the Roman emperor divine honours were the Jews; after his death, his pretensions were re-interpreted as typical of the madness of a tyrant.

Once Gemellus had been removed, the only serious source of instability lay in the absence of a direct heir. Caligula first married Lollia Paulina, probably a granddaughter of M. Lollius, an opponent of Tiberius during Augustus' reign. But when no child appeared after a year, he divorced her (she was later to be mentioned as a candidate for the hand of Claudius) and married Milonia Caesonia, who was to present him with a daughter.

But in the meantime it was his sisters who would legally inherit the *domus Caesaris* should anything happen to him. While women could not become emperor, their sons could, or their husbands on their sons' behalf – much as Agrippa or Tiberius had been prospective guardians of Augustus' direct descendants. This ambivalent relationship between Caligula and his sisters lies behind the accusations of incest, an expression of Caligula's concern that their husbands might become political rivals. Other stories about Caligula's sexual aberrations are along the same lines, e.g. that he slept with Livia Orestilla in order to 'control' her marriage to Calpurnius Piso, who was later to head the conspiracy against Nero of AD 65.

On December 15th, 37, Agrippina and her husband Domitius Ahenobarbus produced a threat in the shape of a son, the later emperor Nero. Suetonius' anecdotes reveal Caligula's intense displeasure; fortunately for the little boy, Ahenobarbus' death in 39 removed the danger as far as Caligula was concerned. To minimise the threat presented by Drusilla, Caligula put an end to her marriage to Lucius Cassius Longinus, and gave her instead to Marcus Aemilius Lepidus, son of the consul of AD 6 whom Tacitus had described as *capax imperii*. Caligula trusted Lepidus (they were accused of being homosexual lovers), but it is no exaggeration to say that Drusilla will have been even more use to him after her death on June 10th, 38. She was deified as the goddess Panthea.

There is no need to postulate any 'oriental' element in her cult. Nor is there much evidence to ascribe to Caligula the intention to turn Rome into an 'oriental' or absolute monarchy. Caligula did count a number of Hellenistic rulers among his *amici*, bestowing kingdoms upon the likes of Cotys in Lesser Armenia, Polemo in Pontus,

Rhoemetalces in eastern Thrace, Antiochus in Commagene, and Agrippa in Palestine; some of them were said to be descendants of Mark Antony, and therefore related to Caligula (Ptolemy, the king of Mauretania, was a son of Cleopatra's daughter Cleopatra Selene). But that does not prove any grandiose plan to bring together Greek East and Roman West under a Hellenistic divine king.

The birth of a daughter in the summer or autumn of 39 meant that Caligula's sisters (and their husbands) ceased to be supporters and turned into threats that Caligula felt it necessary to eliminate. The exact sequence of events is unclear. There may have been a real conspiracy, as Caligula claimed, perhaps associated with the consuls' mysterious failure to offer prayers for the emperor's safety on August 31st. What is clear is that Caligula removed Lepidus, Agrippina and Livilla from Rome by taking them with him on a sudden and well-organised march to the upper Rhine. There Lepidus was tried and executed; the Senate was sent letters incriminating Agrippina (who was accused of adultery with him) and Julia Livilla, and Caligula dedicated three daggers which he alleged had been intended to be used against him. On October 27th, the Arval Brethren gave thanks for Caligula's delivery.

Caligula used the occasion to remove Lentulus Gaetulicus (whom our sources do not accuse of involvement in the conspiracy) and restore the loyalty and discipline of the Rhine legions. To that end he appointed Galba as governor of Upper Germany, and personally led a number of successful military expeditions across the river, following in the footsteps of his father and grandfather. Caligula spent the winter at Lyon, making plans to achieve more spectacular glory: the conquest of Britain. An appeal by a son of Cunobelinus, Adminius, to be installed as king, gave him an excuse to intervene. Two new legions were raised, named *Primigeniae* in honour of Caligula's daughter, and a lighthouse constructed at Boulogne. All this will have cost money, and we find the standard accusations that Caligula spent the winter confiscating the estates of wealthy Gauls. We may be sceptical. The fact that Caligula had abolished one of the sources of revenue for the military treasury in AD 39 (advertised by coins bearing the legend RCC, 'The Half-Per-Cent Remitted') will have contributed to an excess of expenditure over revenue. Caligula's deposition of King Ptolemy and annexation of Mauretania may have been intended to make good the shortfall (just as the annexation of

Cappadocia in AD 18 had allowed Tiberius to reduce the tax from 1%).

Fig. 9. Copper quadrans, AD 39-40 (Rome). The obverse is inscribed 'Gaius Caesar Augustus, great-grandson of the deified Augustus', and depicts a cap of liberty between the letters S[enatus] C[onsulto]. The reverse gives Caligula's titles, together with the letters RCC (remissa ducentesima) announcing the abolition of the half-per-cent sales tax.

In spite of the massive preparations, the invasion never took place; perhaps the Britons sent the required tribute. Ancient sources pour scorn on the whole operation, suggesting that the troops mutinied, or were ordered to collect sea-shells. If that story was true, it was perhaps actually intended as a sign of Caligula's success in dominating the far side of the Ocean, like his ancestor Julius Caesar.

Chapter 9
The Fall of Caligula

The execution of Lepidus and the exile of Agrippina and Julia Livilla together with supporters such as Seneca led to a cooling in relations between Caligula and the elite. It was not Caligula's fault that the man appointed to share the consulship of AD 40 with him should have died just before taking office. The year began without a consul; no appointment could be made without consulting Caligula, who was a week's journey away in Lyon, and was reputed to have asked why his horse Incitatus had not been appointed.

When Caligula returned to Italy after his victory over the Ocean, he stayed outside Rome for three months. These were summer months, not the most pleasant time to be in Rome; there is no need to assume that he was afraid of facing the Senate. Although there had been several suicides and exilings after Lepidus' alleged conspiracy, there is little evidence that the opposition to Caligula was widespread, or that a coup could have been expected.

Caligula was killed, and his wife Caesonia and baby daughter brutally murdered, on January 24th AD 41, by a group of disgruntled officers led by Cassius Chaerea, resentful at being involved in Caligula's attacks on his own family. Two candidates for the succession immediately presented themselves, Marcus Vinicius and Claudius; the speed with which they acted does not prove that either of them had known of Chaerea's plans. Death could come suddenly to political leaders even more frequently than it does now, and potential successors always had to be ready to stake their claim.

Marcus Vinicius had the better claim to inherit the household of Caesar. Under Roman law, the death of the direct heirs – the widow and child – meant that Caligula's sisters were next in line to inherit. Both were in exile; Agrippina was a widow, so there was no-one to put forward the claims of the three-year-old Ahenobarbus (Nero). Julia Livilla was in exile, but her husband Marcus Vinicius was in Rome. He appeared before the Senate to ask for his claim to be confirmed.

Although the idea that at the death of an emperor 'sovereignty' returned to the Senate is a nineteenth-century fiction (as indeed is the whole idea that there was such a thing as a formal constitution at Rome), the deeply held republican conviction that senators ought to have freedom of speech now played a decisive role. At two meetings of the Senate, the presiding consul Q. Secundus Pomponius, instead of acclaiming Vinicius as emperor, invited consideration of other candidates, Annius Vinicianus and Valerius Asiaticus, whose claims to head the *domus Caesaris* were tenuous in the extreme (Asiaticus was married to a sister of Lollia Paulina).

In the meantime Claudius had acted decisively. Later tradition, beginning with Seneca's *Apocolocyntosis*, depicts him as a fool who was accidentally discovered by a guardsman hiding in the palace. Whatever the truth of the story, Claudius went to the praetorian camp, where he was acclaimed emperor; he felt himself secure enough to act out a *recusatio*, the ritual pretence that he did not want to accept the honour. Claudius took the title Caesar – not an assertion of posthumous adoption, for which there was no legal procedure at Rome, but rather an example of the common habit of including in one's own name as a mark of respect the name of the person whose property one had inherited.

As Caligula's uncle, Claudius' claim to inherit was weaker than Julia Livilla's. But another principle of Roman law must be taken into account, that of *possessio*. As we have seen (ch. 4), Roman (praetorian) law recognised as owner whoever had prior possession, until such time as a better claim was proved in court. Once Claudius had *possessio* of the *domus Caesaris*, Vinicius could only lawfully dislodge him by means of a successful lawsuit. It is hardly surprising that he preferred to withdraw his claim.

Claudius' accession was not therefore unlawful, or achieved by violence. Nor should the emphasis on 'liberty' in the debates which took place in the Senate on January 24th and 25th be taken to imply that Claudius was hostile to the Senate. So long as it was unclear who was in control of the *domus Caesaris*, senators could only avoid expressing support for the wrong man by using the language of republicanism. In the end the Senate had no choice but to recognise Claudius.

Nor was Claudius a 'representative' of the army; he happened to be the candidate who, quite properly, chose to ask the praetorians for their support first. He remained acutely conscious of his debt to

Fig. 10. Denarius, AD 41-2 (Rome). Claudius clasps the hand of a representative of the praetorian guard: PRAETOR[iani] RECEPT[i in fidem], i.e. 'The Praetorians have been received (into Claudius' trust)'.

them: Dio tells us that throughout his reign, he continued to pay them 100 sesterces annually. Coins depict Claudius holding a guardsman by the hand, with the various inscriptions 'Loyalty' (FIDES), 'Commander Received' (IMPER. RECEPT.) and 'Praetorians Received' (PRAETOR. RECEPT.). The praetorians were of course only part of the army. January is a bad time for communication, and there were powerful men in command of provincial armies who might feel that they had opinions on the issue. They included Galba in Upper Germany, Aulus Plautius in Pannonia, Camillus Scribonianus in Dalmatia, and Appius Junius Silanus in Tarraconensis.

Chapter 10
A Weak Emperor

Although Caligula was remembered by history as a wicked tyrant, Claudius had to represent himself as his heir and avenger: Chaerea and the other assassins were executed. Although some of Caligula's coins were defaced, Claudius' public statements indicating a new beginning went no further than those Caligula had made four years earlier. Coins bore the legend 'For Citizens Saved' (OB CIVES SERVATOS) and 'Augustan Freedom' (LIBERTAS AUGUSTI); others depicted Claudius' relatives in order to publicise his legitimacy – his parents Drusus and Antonia, his brother Germanicus, his grandmother Livia. Exiles such as Julia Livilla and Agrippina were allowed home.

But Claudius' position was much weaker than Caligula's had been. Some rivals, such as Vinicius, allowed themselves to be conciliated for a time (he was to be consul in AD 45). The governor of Tarraconensis, Marcus Appius Junius Silanus, was parted from his army to marry Claudius' mother-in-law, Domitia Lepida. But these and many others had to be executed in due course, often after a private hearing in the emperor's household court; Seneca's *Apocolocyntosis* refers to thirty-five senators and over 200 equestrians. An immediate threat came from Caligula's sisters. Julia Livilla had to be exiled again, and then executed. Agrippina wished to re-marry. She suggested Galba, but he was far too powerful already to be allowed to become the guardian of her son Ahenobarbus (the later Nero). Claudius allowed her to marry Sallustius Passienus Crispus, adopted son of a close adviser to Augustus, and previously the husband of Agrippina's sister-in-law Domitia. He was granted a second consulship in 44, and died soon after (according to Suetonius, poisoned by Agrippina).

A year before his accession, Claudius' (third) wife Valeria Messallina had borne him a daughter, Octavia; and on February 12th, 41, there was a son, later re-named Britannicus. While these children strengthened Claudius' position, they also gave their potential guardians room for manoeuvre. A conflict between Messallina and Junius Silanus, now the children's step-grandfather, was resolved by

Silanus' execution. Messallina was later accused of responsibility for many other executions during these years, sometimes no doubt justly: Tiberius' granddaughter Julia, wife of Rubellius Blandus, was killed in AD 43. AD 47 saw the execution of Gnaeus Pompeius Magnus and his father, Marcus Licinius Crassus Frugi, greatly honoured by Claudius for military operations in Mauretania – not because they were descended from two powerful families of the late republic, but because Pompeius was the husband of Claudius' daughter Antonia (see Stemma III). Messallina did not want anyone she had not chosen herself to rule if Claudius should die before Britannicus reached adulthood.

Her solution was to engage Octavia, aged two or three in AD 43, to Lucius Junius Silanus Torquatus, aged 16: as a great-grandson of Augustus, he would have a good claim to succeed Claudius when the time came. He was made *praefectus urbi feriarum latinarum causa*. In 45, he distributed largesse to the people on Claudius' behalf. In 48, he was appointed *praetor peregrinus*, 10 years before the normal age. His brother Marcus was consul in 46; his sister Junia Calvina married Lucius Vitellius, son of Claudius' principal supporter, who became consul in 48.

Claudius did what he could to win the support of the people. His public works included draining the Fucine Lake, constructing the Claudian aqueduct (and providing a second gang of workmen to look after it), and developing the harbour facilities at Ostia to improve the regularity of Rome's corn supplies. An inscription advertises the claim that he 'freed the city from flooding' by the canal link with Ostia. To show his concern for the corn-supply, he instituted an imperial procurator to oversee it. He may have introduced a new system of distributing the corn dole to put an end to the start-of-month crush. Coins advertised the 'Augustan Harvest', CERES AUGUSTA.

There were some other changes, too. Four of the quaestors were released from their archaic functions outside Rome (possibly so that they would spend money providing games in the capital); and the State treasury (*Aerarium*) was transferred from two of the praetors to the supervision of two quaestors appointed by the emperor for a three-year period. Our ancient sources, while making fun of Claudius' interest in the law courts, make it clear that he realised that judicial arbitration was one of the emperor's most important duties. But Claudius' administrative changes should not be seen as part of a systematic and far-sighted policy of reform, or centralisation. They

Fig. 11. Silver dish from Aquileia, now in Vienna. Claudius, represented as Triptolemus, sacrifices to Ceres, the provider of grain.

were reactions to particular crises, a sign of Claudius' weakness rather than strength.

Nor are later accusations that Claudius depended too much on his freedmen indications of a policy of concentrating power in an imperial 'chancellery'. Before he became emperor, Claudius had known nothing of the workings of the imperial household; so he depended for advice on the key *liberti* who knew how it worked, like Polybius and Narcissus, as well as Marcus Antonius Pallas, inherited from his mother's household. For a weak man to be ruled by his slaves, or wives (Messallina, Agrippina), is a *topos* (commonplace) of literary invective.

Although Claudius was repaid for the favours he distributed to senators as well as to client kings like Herod Agrippa by being acclaimed *pater patriae* on January 12th, 42, this did not prevent a rebellion by the governor of Dalmatia, Camillus Scribonianus (son of one of Tacitus' *capaces imperii* of AD 14). It was said that Claudius was so frightened that he contemplated resigning his office. But Scribonianus' two legions remained loyal to Claudius, and Scribonianus killed himself. It was thought that he was acting on behalf of conspirators in Rome: Annius Vinicianus, whose name had been discussed in the senatorial debate following Caligula's death, and Pomponius Secundus, the consul who had presided at that debate, were among those executed.

Claudius thought it necessary to hold consular office for a third time in 43. To strengthen his support in the army, soldiers were granted the privileges of married men. Claudius had himself acclaimed *imperator* twenty-seven times during his reign, more than any other emperor. In the early years of his reign, Suetonius Paulinus (cos. 41) and Antonia's father-in-law Marcus Crassus Frugi (cos. 27) completed the annexation of Mauretania, left over from Caligula's execution of king Ptolemy. Lycia was annexed as a province in 43. But this does not imply a conscious 'policy' of expansion, in opposition to Augustus' deathbed advice to Tiberius. Expansion was only permitted where it strengthened Claudius. When Gnaeus Domitius Corbulo, half-brother of Caligula's third wife, wished to pacify Frisia, he was not allowed to do so.

Claudius needed to win military glory in person. To achieve that, he revived Caligula's plan to invade Britain; this would have the additional advantage of removing part of the over-powerful Rhine army, now consisting of ten legions. The legate of Pannonia, Aulus Plautius, was put in command; he was married to a sister of Lucius Vitellius (cos. 34 and 43), and both could be trusted. Vitellius controlled Rome in the emperor's absence. Anyone else who mattered had to accompany Claudius, partly to prevent any coup in his absence, and partly so that they could be granted triumphal *ornamenta* and would thus be beholden to the emperor's *gratia*. They included Marcus Vinicius, Passienus Crispus, and Valerius Asiaticus; when Galba claimed to be ill, the whole expedition had to be postponed so that he would not have an excuse for staying behind.

The victory was prestigious: commemorative coins were struck, and a submissive 'Bretannia' appears on sculpture honouring the *domus* as far away as at Aphrodisias in Asia. But the apparent symbols of success – a fourth consulship in 47, a census in 47 which included the symbolic extension of the city limits (*pomerium*), and a new round

Fig. 12. Gold aureus, AD 46-7 (Lyon). The triumphal arch celebrating Claudius' victory over the Britons, DE BRITANN[is]. A similar coin had already been struck commemorating his father Drusus' victory over the Germans in the time of Augustus.

of Centennial Games (*Ludi saeculares*), could not hide continuing weakness. In 46, Marcus Vinicius had to be executed, and one of Asinius Gallus' sons exiled; another son, Servius Asinius Celer, was executed in 47, as was Valerius Asiaticus. Gnaeus Pompeius Magnus, husband of Claudius' daughter Antonia, was also killed, together with his parents.

After her fall in AD 48, Messallina could be blamed for all these deaths. If she was clearing the ground for the succession of her own children (with or without the young Silanus), it would also have been to her advantage to find a more pliant husband than Claudius to be emperor until Britannicus came of age. Her choice fell on Gaius Silius (cos. 46). Ancient accounts of their conspiracy make it sound like a farce; but there can be no doubt that, in Claudius' absence at Ostia, Messallina repudiated the emperor and formally married Silius. Silius as emperor would have meant the end of Claudius' freedmen as well as of himself; the freedman Narcissus acted quickly to see that the praetorians executed Messallina and all the others involved.

Chapter 11
Claudius and Agrippina

Messallina's attempt to replace Claudius with Gaius Silius showed how dispensable Claudius was, but it was also the last plot against him. It gave his advisers the opportunity to strengthen his position by means of a new matrimonial alliance with Caligula's surviving sister Agrippina (who was also Claudius' niece). In a parody of an epic council-of-war, Tacitus puts the case for different women into the mouths of freedmen at a meeting of Claudius' domestic *consilium*. There was Aelia Paetina, one of Claudius' previous wives and the mother of Antonia; Lollia Paulina, who had been Caligula's second wife, and perhaps a step-great-granddaughter of Augustus; and Agrippina, another great-granddaughter of Augustus, supported by Marcus Antonius Pallas (Claudius' mother, the younger Antonia, who had given him his freedom, had been Agrippina's grandmother). Tacitus assigns Narcissus the role of pointing out that a marriage to Agrippina meant giving her son Ahenobarbus precedence over Messallina's son Britannicus.

The wedding took place on January 1st, AD 49. It was preceded by the abdication from his praetorship and suicide of Lucius Junius Silanus; he no longer had any role to play in the succession. Claudius' loyal supporter Vitellius had to uncouple himself from the Silani. He accused Silanus of incest with his sister Junia Calvina (wife of Vitellius' own son Lucius). He had also persuaded the Senate that it was not incest for the emperor to marry his own niece. Vitellius died suddenly soon after. One consequence of Agrippina's rise was that those who had insulted her in the past disappeared from view for the next ten years: they included Galba and Vespasian.

As Agrippina's husband, there was now no longer any doubt about Claudius' legitimacy, or about the succession. Lucius Domitius Ahenobarbus was adopted as Nero Claudius Caesar on February 25th, 50. The imperial favour shone on Agrippina's supporters from the western provinces. L. Annaeus Seneca (from Corduba) was appointed as Nero's tutor, Sextus Afranius Burrus (from Vaison) as Praetorian Prefect (once her son had become emperor, they were to prove more loyal to him than to herself). Her birthplace Cologne was re-named *Colonia Claudia Ara Agrippinensium* in her honour. In 51, Nero came of age; Britannicus was still only ten. It was Nero who was singled out as the successor by becoming *princeps iuventutis*. In 53, he married Octavia (who had to be adopted into another family to make this legal), and was allowed to address the Senate.

Fig. 13. Nero as a child (note the bulla round his neck) delivers a speech (Louvre, Paris).

There continued to be the usual minor problems – corn riots in 51, and hostilities against Parthia when the Parthian king Vologaesus placed his brother Tiridates on the throne of Armenia. And Britannicus had his supporters: the freedman Narcissus, and his grandmother Domitia Lepida. In 54, Agrippina had her condemned on a charge of allowing her slave herdsmen to roam out of control. If Britannicus were to be a threat to Nero – and there was talk about Claudius promising the Romans a 'real Caesar' – he could only become one after he had put on the adult toga. That would not happen until after his fourteenth birthday on February 12th, 55.

Claudius died from eating mushrooms on the previous October 13th. His death was highly opportune for Agrippina and Nero (for instance, Narcissus happened to be away at the time), and the ancient sources agree that he was poisoned. Nevertheless food poisoning was nothing unusual in the unhygienic conditions of antiquity. Claudius was sixty-three, and had long been ill; his death may have been natural.

Chapter 12
Nero's 'Five Good Years'

At the moment of Claudius' death, Nero had an unchallengeable claim to succeed him. Through his mother, he was the legitimate heir of Caligula, and a great-great-grandson of Augustus himself. In addition, he was Claudius' adopted son, and the husband of Claudius' daughter Octavia, a great-great-grand-niece of Augustus. Claudius had marked him out as his successor by appointing him as 'Prefect of the City for the Duration of the Latin Festival' in AD 51, and the Senate had granted him the privilege of holding a consulship as soon as he reached the age of twenty (in AD 58). In spite of Tacitus' insinuation, the praetorians could not possibly have acclaimed Britannicus as their commander: in October 54, he was still a child, as Tiberius Gemellus had been in 37.

While there was felt to be no need to enquire after Claudius' own wishes as expressed in his will, he was declared a god and voted a temple and cult. This strengthened the prestige of his adopted son Nero, but also that of Britannicus. Should Agrippina feel dissatisfied with the way she was being treated by Nero and his advisers Seneca and Burrus, Britannicus might make a more pliant emperor. And there were other relatives who might be brought forward as candidates by anyone dissatisfied with Nero: most conspicuously, Tiberius' great-grandson Rubellius Plautus. Alternatives to Nero also included a son of Domitia Lepida, Faustus Cornelius Sulla Felix, the second husband of Claudius' daughter Antonia. And grand-children of Julia the Younger survived, the brothers and sisters of the unfortunate Lucius Junius Silanus.

The immediate threat came from Britannicus. Seneca and Burrus were unhappy about the highly visible role Agrippina wished to play: her image appeared alongside her son's on coins, and she made appearances on state occasions. She was accused of attempting to bring them into line by threatening to replace Nero with Britannicus; he would have reached an age to put on the adult toga in February or March 55. While there is no evidence that Britannicus' sudden death before that could happen involved Seneca or Burrus, it

Fig. 14. Gold aureus, AD 54 (Lyon; similar coins struck at Rome). 'Agrippina Augusta, wife of the deified Claudius, mother of Nero Caesar' is given equal prominence with her son.

certainly clarified matters. A personal enemy of Agrippina, Junia Silana (probably a sister of Caligula's first wife), now felt strong enough to accuse her of plotting to make Rubellius Plautus emperor; although she was not believed, Agrippina's loss of influence is illustrated by the disappearance of her portrait from the coinage.

Seneca and Burrus consolidated their hold over the government. Claudius' household treasurer (*a rationibus*), Marcus Antonius Pallas, was dismissed. Friends and relatives of Seneca and Burrus from Spain and Narbonensis were awarded consulships and appointed to provincial governorships, e.g. Seneca's brother-in-law Pompeius Paulinus (from Arles) and Lucius Duvius Avitus (from Vaison, Burrus' home town), who succeeded each other as legates of Lower Germany; the loyalty of the Rhine legions – where Agrippina's memory, and support, were strong – was crucial. Attempts were also made to buttress Nero's prestige with the army in general: a minor campaign in Armenia under the command of Corbulo resulted in his first military salutation in 55. The founding of veteran settlements at Capua and Nuceria in 57 also expressed the need to maintain the support of the army.

There was general agreement amongst senatorial writers that Nero's reign began well. Early in Trajan's reign, there was talk of a '*quinquennium Neronis*', a period of five years when the Roman empire had been particularly fortunate. In late antiquity, historians mistakenly took this to refer to the military victories of Corbulo in the 60s, or to Nero's vast building programme (both expensive and in fact sources of his later unpopularity). One likely interpretation is that the term was coined by writers under the Flavians to explain why the Stoic hero Thrasea Paetus was willing to play a full part in public life during the five years up to Agrippina's murder in AD 59. The fact that so many prominent Flavian supporters (including Vespasian) had served the 'tyrant' for many years was an embarrassment.

There is unmistakable evidence that Nero respected constitutional proprieties – and the honour of the Senate – during these years. No senator lost his life until AD 62, a remarkable contrast to the early years of Claudius. Between AD 54 and 64, for the first time since the minting of gold and silver had been taken over by the emperor late in Augustus' reign, *aurei* and *denarii* bear the legend 'By Order of the Senate', EX S[enatus] C[onsulto]. In 56 Nero accepted the title *pater patriae*, but in 58 he declined an offer of the novel title 'perpetual consul', *consul perpetuus* (perhaps because he felt that it would prevent him from being a *consul ordinarius* again). He intervened in debates, sometimes without waiting to be briefed – on one occasion, he proposed the (entirely unrealistic) abolition of provincial taxes (*vectigalia*). It would be mistaken to interpret this as an indication of a liberal (or any other) 'economic policy'; what it illustrates is the arbitrariness of a Caesar's exercise of favour (*gratia*), something well described in the *De Clementia*, a pamphlet on imperial clemency addressed to Nero by Seneca in AD 55.

Nero sought popularity with the people as well as with the elite. He provided highly expensive spectacles; his reign sees the spread of stone amphitheatres throughout Italy. This was one respect where the personal preferences of an emperor became important. Nero was keen to win respect as a performer in his own right (cf. his reported last words, 'What an artist I was!'). But while the personal participation of members of the aristocracy in athletic or literary competitions was an accepted feature of Greek culture, it horrified Romans of all social classes. At first, Nero was wise enough only to perform in private, e.g. at Greek-style games celebrating the shaving of his beard in 59 (the Juvenilia). It was not until 64 that he appeared in public in the still essentially Greek city of Naples.

Only in later Flavian propaganda was the death of Agrippina in AD 59 interpreted as a turning-point in Nero's reign, an act of unforgivable wickedness typical of a tyrant. In fact, it seems to have made little difference to Nero's popularity at the time. What happened is unclear: Nero's wish to divorce Octavia and marry Poppaea Sabina, the wife of his friend M. Salvius Otho, seems to have been opposed by Agrippina (who pointed out that Octavia, once divorced, would become a focus of opposition). Then Agrippina suffered shipwreck in the Bay of Naples as she was returning home from dinner with her son; the shipwreck may have been an accident, or arranged by Nero to frighten her. Certainly neither Seneca nor Burrus knew anything about it. But when Agrippina accused her son of trying to kill her, he panicked, and ordered her execution. The Senate was plausibly informed that she had sent a freedman to try to assassinate Nero.

The execution of Agrippina did not weaken Nero in the eyes of most senators. Although he immediately sent Otho off to govern Lusitania, thus facilitating access to Poppaea, he did not feel strong enough to divorce Octavia. In the meantime, Seneca and Burrus strengthened his position (and theirs) by sending possible rivals into exile whenever the opportunity presented itself: Sulla Felix had already gone to Marseilles in 58, and the appearance of a comet in 60 – taken as a sign of political turmoil – meant that Rubellius Plautus could be persuaded to retire to his estates in Asia. Servius Sulpicius Galba was sent to govern Tarraconensis – an honourable way of removing a potential opponent.

Chapter 13

The Fire and its Aftermath

In spite of Agrippina's execution, Nero continued to be popular with the people, and accepted by the Senate; but all was not well. His building programmes, and his spectacles, were expensive. Initially it was only the tax-payers in the provinces who suffered. In Britain, imperial procurators took possession of the property which Prasutagus, king of the Iceni, had left to Nero jointly with his own two daughters. Their efficiency was such that the Iceni rebelled under the leadership of Prasutagus' widow, Boudicca. Cassius Dio, preserving a tradition hostile to Seneca, says that a significant additional complaint was the philosopher's wish to call in loans of 40 million sesterces which the Britons had had to borrow at high rates of interest in order to pay Roman taxes. The rebellion was so serious that Nero was reported to have considered evacuating the island.

An additional strain was put on imperial resources by the cost of campaigns in the east. In AD 60, Corbulo installed a Roman client-king, Tigranes V, on the throne of Armenia. In the following year Tigranes unwisely invaded Parthia, and in order to prevent a full-scale war breaking out, Corbulo had to remove him. In 62, an attempt by the new legate of Cappadocia, Caesennius Paetus, to impose Roman authority resulted in the humiliation of his army at Rhandeia. Corbulo, given general command over the eastern armies, negotiated a diplomatic compromise in 63 which gave the throne of Armenia to a Parthian candidate, Tiridates, but on condition that he went to Rome to receive his diadem from Nero in person (this spectacle was enacted in 66).

In 62, a commission of three consulars was appointed to review tax-collecting procedures. This is not necessarily a sign that Nero and his advisers were concerned by discontent with, let alone the injustice of, the way taxes were being exacted in the provinces, but rather by a serious disparity between revenue and expenditure. Our sources report widespread confiscations, including that of the estates of six equestrians who between them owned half of 'Africa' (more realistically, the Bagradas valley which produced a considerable proportion of the province's grain surplus). As we have seen in the case of Caligula, the *topos* of unjust prosecutions leading to the confiscation of the property of the rich was a typical charge levelled against wicked tyrants. But there is other evidence for the government's financial embarrassment. The weight of gold and silver coins declines throughout the period when Seneca and Burrus were in control. Gold *aurei* drop from 7.7/7.6 grammes to 7.4/7.25; silver *denarii* from 3.65/3.55 to 3.5/3.2. Then, at some point in the mid 60s, there was a major currency reform: a pound of gold now made 45 *aurei* instead of 42, and there were 96 *denarii* to the pound of silver rather than 84. A new series of sestertius-types began to be struck from AD 64.

It is tempting to see some of the political events of AD 62 as a consequence of these administrative problems. In that year Seneca retired from political life (though that was what a Roman senator had traditionally been allowed to do at the age of 65); Burrus died, to be succeeded as Praetorian Prefect by Ofonius Tigellinus. Later Tigellinus was to become a useful scapegoat for the bloody repression of Nero's last three years, and that is how he has gone down in the historiographical tradition. But that may not be entirely fair. Tigellinus was a protégé of Seneca's, and there is no evidence that his appointment signifies a new political direction. On the other hand, later tradition may be right in thinking that Nero, now in his twenties, wanted more scope to indulge his personal tastes. These included divorcing Octavia (the execution of the exiled potential rivals Sulla Felix and Rubellius Plautus prepared the way for the divorce). What Nero may not have envisaged was that popular demonstrations occurred at Rome in Octavia's support; they frightened him into having her executed on July 9th, 62. Two years later, one of the last legitimate descendants of Augustus, Decimus Junius Silanus Torquatus, was forced to commit suicide.

Nero duly married Poppaea, who gave birth to a daughter in January 63; but the girl, Claudia Augusta, only lived for a few months. The following year saw a much more memorable catastrophe. The fire which raged for nine days and destroyed most of the centre of Rome began on the night of July 18/19th, 64. As the *pater patriae* who was ultimately responsible for the well-being of his people, the emperor was inevitably blamed for the disaster: hence stories about his playing the lyre, when in fact it is clear that he personally took what action he could to prevent the fire from spreading. Nero tried to divert popular resentment against himself towards the Christians, who were executed in the manner appropriate to arsonists. But while the fire itself, and the attempt to blame the Christians, may have made him unpopular among some sections of the urban population, Nero compounded it with a grandiose reconstruction programme which alienated the elite. Quite apart from its cost, Nero's plan for a vast new palace (parts of which survive as the 'Golden House') required the expropriation of sites on which many senatorial families had had their houses, some for generations (recent excavations between the Palatine and forum have unearthed some of these palaces, destroyed in the fire).

To pay for his new palace, Nero ordered the confiscation of temple treasures in the provinces. In May 66 the procurator of Judaea, Gessius Florus, arrived in Jerusalem with a demand for 40 gold talents to cover unpaid taxes. Florus forcibly extracted 17 talents from the Temple treasury, thus sparking off the most serious rebellion since the imposition of Roman rule. The legate of Syria, Cestius Gallus, intervened, but for some unknown reason retreated in November 66 without curbing the rebellion (he may have died of natural causes).

In Rome too the opposition turned to the use of force. Since Nero had killed almost all legitimate claimants to head the household of the Caesars, the plotters had to select as their candidate Gaius Calpurnius Piso, whose link with the imperial family was extremely tenuous: perhaps he was related to Julius Caesar's wife Calpurnia. It is not clear how much support the Pisonian conspiracy had; but its detection scared Nero, and resulted in executions, forced suicides, and exile. For Nero, it was the start of a vicious circle in which the suppression of opposition evoked even more widespread opposition. Former advisers such as Seneca and Petronius Arbiter had to commit suicide. Gaius Cassius Longinus, husband of Augustus' great-granddaughter Junia Lepida, was amongst those exiled. Rubellius Plautus' father-in-law Antistius Vetus was executed. Needless to say, Tacitus spares no details of these massacres; the surviving narrative of the *Annals* breaks off in the middle of the account of the forced suicides of the Stoic 'heroes' Thrasea Paetus and Barea Soranus.

The death of Poppaea deprived Nero of the likelihood of an immediate heir. (We need not believe the *topos* that, like a typical tyrant, Nero had killed her by kicking her when pregnant.) He first tried unsuccessfully to persuade Claudius' surviving daughter

Antonia to marry him. Later he strengthened his position by marrying Statilia Messalina, descended from two of Augustus' most important generals.

Nero recognised the need to bolster his military prestige. Much was made of the visit of Tiridates to Rome in 66 to receive the throne of Armenia. Coins proclaimed the 'Victory of Augustus' (VICTORIA AUGUSTI) and 'The Closing of the Temple of Janus with Peace attained by Land and Sea' (PACE P[OPULI] R[OMANI] TERRA MARIQUE PARTA IANUM CLUSIT). The title GERMANICUS

Fig. 15. Brass sestertius, AD 64-5 ((Lyon). Nero shuts the Temple of Janus.

emphasises respect for the military. Plans seem to have been made for an imperial military expedition to the Caspian Gates (the Caucasus), possibly to prevent nomadic tribes such as the Alani from threatening the peace of both the Parthian and Roman empires. A new legion was raised, and the XIVth withdrawn from Britain in preparation for this campaign. On the way east, Nero visited Greece; he seems genuinely to have felt that he could enhance his prestige even more by showing that he was a great athlete and musician. The Olympic Games had to be re-scheduled to enable him to compete. While Roman writers portray his attitude as ludicrous, there is no doubt that it made him genuinely popular with at least some Greeks.

The enforced suicide of Corbulo was another sign that Nero was well aware how crucial military prestige was. While on the way to

Greece, Corbulo's son-in-law Annius Vinicianus was detected in a conspiracy at Beneventum. Although Corbulo had made no move to oppose Nero (Tiridates, in Rome, had referred to him as Nero's 'most loyal slave'), his success as a soldier was too great for Nero to tolerate. When in February 67 he had to deal with the Jewish rebellion, Nero thought it safest to make not one, but two appointments in the East, Licinius Mucianus as legate of Syria, and Flavius Vespasianus to take command in the field. The rivalry between the two would effectively prevent either from threatening Nero.

THE CIVIL WARS

Chapter 14
Power Passes to Sulpicius Galba

The events of AD 69 are narrated in the surviving first three books of Tacitus' *Histories*; the account of the equally momentous events of the year 68 at the end of the *Annals* is lost. Plutarch's *Lives* of Galba and Otho are no substitute, and Cassius Dio survives only in extract. Consequently there are a number of questions which we do not have enough evidence about to resolve. Perhaps the most important is just why Nero lost his nerve.

The projected military expedition to the Caspian Gates never took place. By late 67, the extent of discontent both in the provinces and among the elite at Rome caused such concern to the officials of Nero's household that Helius, the freedman who had been left in charge at Rome, himself travelled to Greece in January 68 to persuade Nero to return at once. Imperial procurators in a number of provinces had reported receiving or intercepting letters urging rebellion in the name of Gaius Julius Vindex, the legate of Gallia Lugdunensis. When he reached Naples, Nero heard that Vindex had indeed thrown off his allegiance. He was not unduly perturbed. Vindex had few troops, and Nero could take the loyalty of the Rhine legions to the Caesars for granted (both Germanicus and Caligula had commanded them in person). Later, when the Flavians were emperors, the legate of Upper Germany in 68, Verginius Rufus, refused to comment about his loyalties at this time. But Tacitus lets drop the remark that these legions 'were late in abandoning Nero'. Nero took other precautions as well. He gathered an army in northern Italy under the command of Petronius Turpilianus, who had proved a loyal supporter in the suppression of Piso's conspiracy.

Neither Vindex's motives, nor his political programme, can be assessed with certainty. What can be dismissed is the idea – popular in the late nineteenth and early twentieth centuries – that he represented a Gallic 'nationalism' hostile to Rome. Vindex was descended from Aquitanian (Basque) chieftains (although his name is Celtic), and needless to say he made the most of his tribal connections: we are told that many of Galba's Spanish supporters were Basques. We may also assume that inter-tribal rivalry played a role in determining which side different tribes chose to support in the conflict (though we cannot assess the full extent of this). But while Vindex exploited the discontent of the provincials he governed, his coins make it clear that he did this in the name of the Roman elite of which he felt himself a part.

Nero had now survived several years of hostility. Those who opposed him had consequently had to develop an 'ideology' to justify their wish to get rid of him. It was not enough for them to want to replace Nero by someone else; they also had to claim to oppose 'tyranny' in principle. Stoic ideas about just kingship were perhaps less important in this than Roman *exempla* of tyrannicide to be found in histories and in rhetorical textbooks. Vindex's coinage mirrors that of Brutus after Caesar's assassination, with slogans such as 'Jupiter the Liberator', 'Rome Restored', 'The Well-being of the Human Race', and 'Hercules the Champion' (Hercules was a god of justice and social order). 'Mars the Avenger' is represented with the 'Standards of the Roman People', and some coins are issued SPQR, in the name of the Roman Senate and People. In the pamphlets he circulated, Vindex attacked Nero for his public appearances as a lyre-player and charioteer and for his philhellenism in general; he addressed Nero as 'Ahenobarbus', i.e. not a real Caesar at all.

When Caligula was killed in 41, Galba had been in Germany, and the action was in Rome. Now the centre of activity was in a province, indeed nearer to Galba in Tarraconensis than to Nero in Italy. (We may note that when Tacitus said that the events of 68 and 69 showed that an emperor could be made outside Italy, he meant precisely that – not that emperors could be made by the army, or that military support was all that an emperor needed.) Titus Vinius Rufinus, the commander of the VIth legion, stationed in Galba's province, urged him to put forward his claim. Once he had the support of the legate of Lusitania, Salvius Otho, and the governor of Baetica, Caecina Alienus, Galba controlled both a rich source of military recruits, and most of the empire's sources of precious metals. Early in April, he proclaimed himself 'Legate of the Roman Senate and People'. He began to levy additional troops, and to pay them *denarii* with representations of 'The Freedom of the Roman People', 'The Life-force of the Roman People', and with Mars and a liberty-cap. The reverse of his *denarii* advertise 'The Co-operation of the Spanish and Gallic Provinces' (CONCORDIA HISPANIARUM ET

GALLIARUM) and 'The Victory of the Roman People'. These
slogans do not of course permit us to conclude either that Galba
seriously wanted to restore a pluralist republic, or that he had been
the instigator of Vindex's rebellion in Gaul.

*Fig. 16. Brass sestertius, AD 68 (Rome). Galba celebrates his restoration of
'Public Liberty'.*

Galba's bid almost came to nought. At the end of May (perhaps
early June) there was a major battle between Verginius Rufus' Rhine
legions and Vindex's Gaulish volunteers at Besançon; the legions
were victorious, and Vindex committed suicide. Nero had clearly
been right to rely on Rufus' army, though Rufus later had to deny that
he was fighting for Nero, and implausibly pretended that the battle
had been a mistake. Some modern scholars accept this story. But the
fact that instead of waiting for Galba, Vindex had marched north from
Lyon to meet Rufus' army can only mean that he wanted to defeat
Rufus before any more troops loyal to Nero arrived from Italy. At
some point the victorious legions tried unsuccessfully to persuade
Rufus to become emperor. If the story is true, it is most likely to have
happened after they heard of Nero's death: having defeated Galba's
supporters, the Rhine legions had no wish to see Galba as their
commander. Some months later they were more successful in
persuading Vitellius to be their emperor.

The news of Vindex's defeat made Galba contemplate suicide
too. But then news arrived from Rome that Nero had lost his nerve;
it will probably never be possible to understand what went on in his

mind – whether or not, for instance, he had heard of the outcome of the battle of Besançon – but he seems first to have planned to flee to Egypt, and then simply to have allowed control of the praetorian guard and of the imperial household to slip into the hands of the Prefect, Nymphidius Sabinus. On June 9th, the Senate proclaimed that Galba was Caesar and Emperor. Nero fled the city and killed himself.

It was Nymphidius who was actually in control of Rome. He allowed those who claimed to have suffered under Nero to attack some of the freedmen of the *domus Caesaris*, and blamed his colleague as Praetorian Prefect, Tigellinus, for any excesses committed in recent years; Tigellinus happened to be sick and away from Rome, and therefore unable to defend himself. Nymphidius also began to spread the story that he was actually an illegitimate son of Caligula. Conflict between Galba and the men who had joined him in Spain on the one hand, and Nymphidius and the imperial household in Rome on the other, was inevitable.

Chapter 15
Galba's Failure and the Reign of Otho

Galba's recognition as emperor meant that the handful of men of senatorial status who joined him in Spain in the spring of AD 68 were catapulted into prominence. Consequently their jealousies and rivalries also became crucial. Galba was 70, and it could not be assumed that he would live for ever. He had no children. His two principal supporters, Titus Vinius the legate of the VIth legion and Otho legate of Lusitania, came to an agreement: the thirty-seven year-old Otho was to marry Vinius' daughter, and when Galba died, succeed him. Otho's children and successors would thus be Vinius' grandchildren.

Other ambitious men had been quick to support Galba in the hope of preferment. Antonius Primus had been living in exile at Marseille, after being accused of forging a will; Galba had put him in command of his new VIIth legion. At Bonn, the legionary legate Fabius Valens arrested and executed his governor, Fonteius Capito, for 'plotting', i.e. having co-operated with Verginius Rufus. He will have hoped for promotion from Galba, but instead Aulus Vitellius was appointed to be governor of Lower Germany in December 68. At the same time, Galba tried to secure the Upper Rhine army by replacing Verginius Rufus with Hordeonius Flaccus. Caecina Alienus, who had supported Galba from the beginning, was put in charge of the two legions at Mainz.

Galba was also faced with the need to replace other legates. Our sources do not permit us to reconstruct what happened in Africa: at some point Lucius Clodius Macer, the legate of the IIIrd legion stationed in Numidia, struck coins proclaiming his independence of Nero, or Galba, or both, and raised a second legion (his coins bear the legends LEG III LIB[eratrix] AUG[usta] and I MACRIANA LIB[eratrix]). He also seems to have prevented corn supplies from reaching Rome. This was one reason why the people of Rome saw no improvement coming from Nero's fall. There were other reasons. Although he was referred to as Livius to recall the fact that he had

Fig. 17. Silver denarius, AD 68 (Carthage). The obverse bears the head of L. CLODIUS MACER, described on the reverse as PRO PRAE[tor] AFRICAE; the warship indicates Macer's intention to control the Western Mediterranean.

been a protégé of Livia and her relatives, Galba ostentatiously refused to behave as the new head of the household of Caesar. He had Helius, Polyclitus, and some other leading freedmen of Nero's executed; he awarded his own freedmen Icelus and Asiaticus equestrian status. He gave performers meagre tips out of his own household purse, rather than large rewards in his capacity as the new Caesar. A particular insult to the servants of the Caesars was that on his journey from Spain he preferred to dine off his own family dinner plates.

Nymphidius Sabinus made the most of this discontent. It was thought that when Galba reached Rome, he would appoint his own Praetorian Prefect, Cornelius Laco, in Nymphidius' place. It is unclear whether Nymphidius tried to organise a coup, or was merely accused of one by Galba's supporters. In any event Galba's arrival in Italy was bloody – there were executions (including that of Nero's friend Mithridates of Pontus) and suicides; and there was considerable bloodshed when Galba denied legionary (and therefore citizen) status to the *legio I Adiutrix* which Nero had raised from the Misenum marines. Galba seemed to be doing nothing to win the loyalty of either the *domus Caesaris* or the army. By proposing to put on fewer spectacles than Nero had, and setting up a commission of thirty to try to recover some of the gifts distributed by Nero, he alienated the people and the Senate as well. A vendetta against Neronian 'informers' added to the discontent.

Galba will have seen that he would be allowed to continue only as long as there was no obvious successor. His nearest relative was his nephew Publius Cornelius Dolabella; the Germans who traditionally formed the Caesars' private bodyguard assumed that they owed Dolabella special respect, and Galba's displeasure may have partly been caused by his fear that this would only lead to his nephew's early death at the hands of his more powerful supporters. He will have been aware that Titus Vinius and Otho were acting in concert. Vinius' position was emphasised by the consulship he held jointly with Galba from January 69 (the point at which Tacitus' *Histories* begin). The prospect of Vinius and Otho in control did not appeal to their personal enemy Caecina Alienus at Mainz. When Verginius Rufus' old soldiers refused to take the oath to Galba on January 1st, Caecina proposed that they choose a different emperor. Vitellius, the newly appointed legate of Lower Germany, would do.

The thought of having Otho recognised as his successor did not appeal to Galba either: the moment the succession was clear, his presence would no longer be welcome. The news of the rebellion by the Rhine legions probably reached him before his formal adoption of Lucius Calpurnius Piso Frugi Licinianus on January 10th. Galba's choice has mystified scholars who took at face value Tacitus' account, especially the speech in which Galba advocated the principle of adoption, as though turning the imperial office into a sort of life-presidency in which each emperor chose the 'best man' as his successor without regard for kinship (a principle which did not apply even in the period of so-called 'adoptive emperors' in the second century AD). Galba appointed a complete nonentity with no administrative experience (but descended from the brother of Augustus' first wife Scribonia (Stemma III); Piso's brother had been the Gn. Pompeius Magnus married to Claudius' daughter Antonia, and killed by Messallina). We do not even know if Piso had been a senator. It was not so much a choice *for* Piso, as *against* Otho. And perhaps Galba was too fond of Dolabella to put his nephew in danger by proclaiming him his heir.

Otho realised that the adoption of Piso was meant to exclude him, and he responded quickly. Vinius had proved no help to him. Otho won over a number of praetorian tribunes Galba had been unwise enough to dismiss; the praetorian guard had still not been paid the donative of 30000 sesterces promised them by Nymphidius Sabinus, and were prepared to support a new emperor. On January 15th, Galba, Piso, and Vinius (despite his pretence that he was a party to Otho's plot) were assassinated in the forum. The Senate duly recognised the fact that Otho was in control. It may be that Otho only then realised that the Rhine legions had rebelled against Galba. Attempts to negotiate with them proved unsuccessful.

Otho was the first emperor to reach the office by killing his predecessor. He attempted to legitimate his position by emphasising that he was Nero's successor rather than Galba's. Galba's freedman Icelus and Praetorian Prefect Laco were executed. Otho gave support to the story that all the excesses of Nero's later years (when he himself was in Lusitania) could be blamed on the sick Tigellinus, who was also executed. Statues of Poppaea, who had been first Otho's and then Nero's wife, were replaced. Most importantly, Otho planned to marry Statilia Messalina, Nero's last wife and therefore (in the absence of any children) legitimate heir. Men who had held high office under Nero were honoured. In an attempt to mollify the Rhine legions, Verginius Rufus was given a second consulship, and Flavius Sabinus was re-appointed to the post of City Prefect from which Galba had dismissed him. Sabinus' son, whom Galba had prevented from being *consul ordinarius* for 69, was promised a suffect consulship in July/August. Soldiers were rewarded for military activities on the Danube: one was the legionary legate Aurelius Fulvus, whose grandson was to be the emperor Antoninus Pius. Otho was recognised as legitimate head of the *domus Caesaris* throughout the empire. Coins bearing his titles were minted as far away as Antioch, and the legend 'Peace on Earth' (PAX ORBIS TERRARUM) was not unduly optimistic.

Chapter 16
A Military Coup: Vitellius

After a century of peace, Italy saw two bloody civil wars in AD 69. Wars are won by soldiers; and this raises the question of whether the principate was simply a military dictatorship. Roman society had for centuries put great emphasis on military values: emperors were military commanders, and whatever their personal inclinations (cf. Nero), they had to represent themselves as successful soldiers. But that did not mean that the leader of the most powerful group of soldiers could become a legitimate emperor. An emperor might lose his position because he lost a battle, as Otho did, or lost the support of the praetorian guard, as Nero and Galba did; but the failure of Vitellius to maintain the support of governors and procurators throughout the empire shows that military victory was not enough by itself to establish a man as the legitimate emperor.

Galba and Otho won the support of significant groups of soldiers in Rome; Vitellius was proclaimed by an important army group. He was chosen because in January 69 he happened to be the most senior senator in the two Rhine provinces. It is possible that if the Rhine armies had heard of Galba's death before turning to Vitellius, they might have accepted Otho as a legitimate successor to Nero (though the legate at Mainz, Caecina Alienus, was personally hostile to Otho, and careful planning had gone into the pronunciamento). Once they had proclaimed Vitellius, no-one had an interest in avoiding civil war: the rapid promotion of Galba's supporters in the previous year showed how much both officers and soldiers had to gain if their candidate were recognised at Rome. It was well understood that an emperor might be proposed by an army, but could not be made legitimate by an army. An emperor was the head of the household of Caesar, recognised as such by the Senate and people. After his proclamation, Vitellius called himself Germanicus to indicate his special relationship with the Rhine army; he only took the title Augustus in response to popular pressure after he had entered Rome. He refused recognition as Caesar until the last days of his reign, when he realised that he had alienated the dependants of the *domus Caesaris*.

Vitellius' two principal – and rival – supporters were Caecina Alienus and Fabius Valens (who had not received the promotion he expected from Galba). They led their armies towards Italy by separate routes (Tacitus follows pro-Flavian sources in stressing the havoc the troops caused along the way). Vitellius himself was to follow in March. Otho could assume that Caecina's army would not be able to cross the Alpine passes before April; his own forces held the coastal road along the Maritime Alps, and Valens' cavalry units were unable to break through into Italy. The governors of Corsica and the Maritime Alps made the mistake of switching to Vitellius prematurely, and met their deaths. Otho prepared to concentrate a loyal army in northern Italy to do battle in the spring.

But spring came unexpectedly early in 69. Caecina Alienus was able to cross the Great St. Bernard with 18,000 men early in March. Out of rivalry with Valens, Caecina hoped for a quick victory; but he was no match for Otho's units (including Nero's *legio I Adiutrix*). In early April, he was joined at Cremona by Valens. Otho now had to decide whether to wait for the arrival of the legions he had summoned from the Danube before giving battle; that was what his generals (including Suetonius Paulinus) advised. But politically that would have been dangerous. The Vitellians had enough men in Italy to divide their force, and send part of it to occupy Rome. Once Vitellius was recognised in Rome, Otho's rule would be over. Otho decided that he had to fight before waiting for the Pannonian legions, even though two of them had already entered Italy. The battle, usually called the first battle of Cremona or Bedriacum, took place on the 14th of April. Otho lost, and committed suicide on the 16th. Writers otherwise critical of his reign recognised that by doing so he had saved Italy from much further bloodshed.

On the 19th, the Senate met at Rome and formally advised the people to grant Vitellius the *imperium* held by his imperial predecessors. A key role seems to have been played by the City Prefect, Flavius Sabinus, who ordered the execution of Galba's nephew Dolabella (who may have tried to rally Otho's supporters). In addition to his other titles, Vitellius was proclaimed Perpetual Consul, the title Nero had rejected. Our sources do not explain why Vitellius wished to be called Germanicus rather than Caesar. It is possible that he saw himself as founding a new dynasty, entirely unconnected with that of the Caesars. His coins emphasise his descent from Claudius' minister, the censor; they also advertise the existence of Vitellius' children, pointing to future dynastic stability. He betrothed his young daughter to Valerius Asiaticus, the son of the Valerius Asiaticus who had put forward a claim to the imperial office in AD 41; this may have been an attempt to reconstitute the circle of his father's supporters. He also tried to win the support of other political figures, by keeping Flavius Sabinus as Urban Prefect and producing coins honouring his brother Vespasian's successes in Judaea. But he seems not to have seen how important it was to win the loyalty of those client kings, procurators and freedmen who considered themselves the personal dependants of a 'Caesar' rather than officials of whoever held the imperial office.

Fig. 18. Gold aureus, AD 69 (Rome). Vitellius' son and daughter, symbols of future dynastic security, with the caption 'The children of Imperator Germanicus Augustus' (he is not described as 'Caesar').

Chapter 17
Vitellius Defeated

When Nero had appointed Mucianus as legate of Syria and Vespasian to a separate command to suppress the Jewish revolt in AD 67, it was so that friction between the two should prevent either from turning against Nero himself. In the event, both remained loyal to Nero; and neither was seduced by Vitellius' overtures. By 69, most of Judaea except for Jerusalem itself was again under Roman control, and the six legions in Syria and Palestine were available for action against Vitellius' Rhine army.

Had the two eastern legates not thrown off their loyalty to Vitellius, the legions on the Danube would probably have set up yet another candidate. Antonius Primus was still in command of the VIIth legion raised by Galba just a year earlier. The XIIIth legion had been treated with dishonour by the Vitellians after the battle of Cremona (the soldiers had been forced to repair an amphitheatre). In Moesia, the IIIrd *Gallica* and its legate Aurelius Fulvus had been honoured by Otho; that legion had also until recently been part of the Syrian army.

The loyalty of individual procurators to the memory of Nero and Otho was as important as that of the legionaries. In Pannonia, while the governor dithered, it was the imperial procurator Cornelius Fuscus who advocated throwing off allegiance to Vitellius; Fuscus was to become one of the leading ministers of the Flavian emperors up to his death at the hands of the Dacians in 86. But the first move was made by Tiberius Julius Alexander, the Prefect of Egypt. Alexander belonged to the foremost hellenised Jewish family in Egypt (he was a nephew of the philosopher Philo); his father had been a procurator of Claudius' mother Antonia; for several years he had been responsible for Corbulo's commissariat as his *praefectus castrorum*. Alexander was at the centre of the network of Hellenistic princes who saw themselves as the friends and dependants of the Caesars, and had nothing to hope for from a new dynasty headed by Vitellius. On July 1st, Alexander proclaimed Vespasian as his emperor (an account of this proclamation has been found on papyrus). Vespasian had absolutely no legal right to succeed to the *domus Caesaris*. Instead, stories were circulated about oracles which foretold his divinely-approved kingship, how he performed miracles, and of prophecies that a divine king would come out of Palestine to rule the world in justice.

When the news from Alexandria reached Vespasian's army on July 3rd, he was duly acclaimed in Palestine, and soon after also by Mucianus and the Syrian legions. In mid-July, the two legates met at the Roman colony of Berytus (Beirut) to plan the overthrow of Vitellius. Vespasian was to stay behind in the east – and control Rome's corn supply – while Mucianus took most of his army on the long march across Anatolia to the Balkans. We have no indication of what was to happen then; but the imperial freedman Hormus approached the Prefects of both the Italian fleets (at Misenum and Ravenna) on Vespasian's behalf, and it is possible that arrangements were made to bring Mucianus' army across the Adriatic to Brindisi in the spring of AD 70.

Fig. 19. Silver denarius, AD 69-70, perhaps Ephesus. Ceres represents the plenty that the 'harmony of Vespasian's regime', CONCORDIA AUG[usti], will bring about.

Whatever the Flavian plan, events had already moved too fast for it to be put into effect. By the time Mucianus reached the Balkans in September, he found that most of the Danube army had left its posts and followed the VIIth legion, under Antonius Primus, into Italy. Mucianus left his Syrian troops in Moesia to protect the frontier there, and went after Primus. It was essential to ensure that if the Danube army won the war against Vitellius, it did so in the name of Vespasian, and not of some other imperial candidate backed by Primus (Vespasian's brother Sabinus had already had the obvious candidate, Galba's nephew Dolabella, executed). When Primus reached Padua, he showed where his first loyalty lay: he restored busts of Galba. By occupying northern Italy, Primus prevented Vitellius from receiving any further reinforcements from the Rhineland. In association with Hordeonius Flaccus, whom Galba had appointed as legate of Upper Germany, he arranged for Julius Civilis, a Batavian chieftain, to raise a rebellion in the lower Rhineland; the rebels took an oath of loyalty to Vespasian.

It was already clear to some of Vitellius' officers that the failure to win the loyalty of Julio-Claudian procurators and client kings meant that Vitellius' cause was hopeless. Caecina had marched north to oppose Primus' army; he next tried, but failed, to persuade his Vitellian troops to switch to Vespasian; then he fled to the Prefect of the fleet at Ravenna, who had no difficulty in bringing the Adriatic fleet over to the Flavian side. On October 24th, Primus attacked the Vitellian army, devoid of an effective commander. The second battle of Cremona (or Bedriacum) was a bloody affair, described in rhetorical detail by Tacitus, resulting in the burning down of the city itself and the destruction of Vitellius' army. Vitellius' other general, Valens, tried to return to the Rhineland to raise another army, but was arrested by the procurator of Narbonensis and subsequently executed by Primus.

When Otho lost the first battle of Cremona in April, he committed suicide in order to put a swift end to the bloodshed. After the second battle, it took months before all resistance from Vitellius' soldiers was overcome. His supporters had invested so much in his cause that they saw no point in surrendering while their own emperor was still alive. When the Misenum fleet went over to Vespasian in November, Vitellius' brother Lucius occupied Campania, and achieved some military successes there until the end of December. Praetorians loyal to Vitellius held the major road over the Apennines at Narnia until mid-December. Primus made no attempt to advance on Rome – not, perhaps, because he loyally intended to leave that honour to Mucianus, but rather because he hoped to find a relative of Galba whom he could proclaim as his own imperial candidate.

Towards the end of December Vitellius made an effort to surrender by negotiating with the City Prefect, still Flavius Sabinus, Vespasian's elder brother. But when at a public ceremony he handed over his dagger – the Roman general's symbol of command – to the consul Caecilius Simplex, his own troops refused to allow him to abdicate. At this point Petillius Cerealis, a close relative of Vespasian (probably the husband of his deceased daughter Domitilla) who was to become suffect consul in 70 and 74, attempted a sudden raid on Rome in support of the Flavians. He was repulsed, and the irate Vitellians attacked Sabinus and forced him to take refuge on the Capitol. The Flavians defended themselves against Vitellius' supporters by starting fires; the Capitoline temple was destroyed. Sabinus and others met their deaths, although Vespasian's younger son, Domitian, escaped.

It was clear that there could be no negotiated end to hostilities. Antonius Primus had to follow Cerealis with the rest of his army. He entered the city on December 20th; Tacitus claims that the fighting was bloody. Vitellius was killed.

Chapter 18
Legitimacy Restored: Vespasian in Control.

Just like the supporters of Galba and of Vitellius, the group of officers who had come together as the 'Flavian party' (*partes Flavianae*) contained rivals for prestige and power. The great achievement of Licinius Mucianus was not merely that he himself was happy to take the second place behind Vespasian, and spend the rest of his days writing books, but that he managed to prevent such rivalry from destabilising the new regime.

Mucianus reached Rome some days after Primus, and acted swiftly to isolate him. Primus had not so much led his army in support of Vespasian, as against Vitellius. Tacitus suggests that either before or after the occupation of Rome, he tried and failed to persuade Licinius Crassus Scribonianus to become his own puppet emperor. As brother of the Piso adopted by Galba, and the Gn. Pompeius Magnus married to Claudius' daughter Antonia, Crassus had a legitimate claim to head the household of Caesar, unlike Vespasian. Even before his arrival, Mucianus had sent written instructions to the Senate to ensure that Vespasian was duly recognised as Caesar and Augustus, and that the people passed a law voting him all the legal powers that earlier emperors had had (an inscription bearing part of the text of this *lex de Imperio Vespasiani* still exists). While Mucianus arranged for rewards for those who had been a party to Vespasian's own plans – the freedman Hormus was granted equestrian status – Antonius Primus, the man who had actually defeated Vitellius, was eased out of power and never again played a political role. For Vespasian's security, Mucianus arranged for the execution of possible candidates for the imperial office: G.Piso Galerianus (son of the conspirator), and his father-in-law Lucius Piso (cos. 57), current proconsul of Africa. Both were suspect as the husbands of women related to Augustus' first wife Scribonia (see Stemma III).

Mucianus' next problem was to defuse the rivalry between Vespasian's two sons. Titus had won military glory as his father's legate in Judaea (he was to remain behind for the prestige of destroying

Jerusalem that summer). Domitian suspected that he would have little chance of surviving long if his brother ever came to the throne. One option open to him was to win military glory himself by leading the Flavian legions north to deal with the remaining Vitellian units in Gaul, Britain and the Rhineland. Mucianus allowed Domitian to accompany his army as far as Lyon (thus removing him from Rome); but then prevented him from seeing any fighting. Instead of seeking to rival Titus as a soldier, Domitian dedicated himself to literary pursuits, and survived the next eleven years by pretending to have no political ambitions.

Fig. 20. Silver denarius, AD 70 (Rhineland). Coin struck by Julius Classicus, probably to pay Dillius Vocula's legionaries (the reverse refers to the support of the XVth legion). The slogan 'Champion of Freedom', ADSERTOR LIBERTATIS, should be interpreted in Roman constitutionalist, rather than nationalist, terms.

    The failure of the Rhine legions to accept Vespasian after Vitellius' death proved a major embarrassment to the Flavians. To avoid giving the impression that Vespasian had been supported by Batavians and (some) Gauls, while the citizen legions and (other) Gauls continued to constitute a 'Vitellian' force, Flavian historians had to re-write the story of Civilis' rebellion against Vitellius as though it was a rebellion by provincials against Roman rule. That is the story as Tacitus tells it in the *Histories*. But if Civilis was a traitor, he was a traitor only to Vitellius, not to Rome. At the behest of Antonius Primus, he took the oath to Vespasian and besieged a Vitellian legion at Vetera (Xanten). Tacitus misleadingly suggests that by the beginning of 70, the legions too had taken the oath of loyalty to Vespasian. In fact, the legate of Upper Germany, Hordeonius Flaccus (who had supported Civilis' action) was killed by his troops when he tried to administer the oath. A pro-Vitellian legate, Dillius Vocula, came to the help of the soldiers at Vetera; when the legionaries tried to evacuate the camp there and march south in March 70, they were massacred by Civilis' Batavians (Tacitus emphasises the presence of Germanic warriors from across the Rhine among Civilis' soldiers).

Fig. 21. Silver denarius, AD 70 (Rhineland). Classicus advertises the support of Gaul (GALLIA) and the loyalty (FIDES) of the Roman army. The boar was a Roman legionary emblem.

The leaders of a number of Gallic tribes also remained loyal to the Vitellian cause. When Mucianus sent Petillius Cerealis north with the Flavian army in the spring of 70, their opposition could be re-interpreted as a tribal uprising. But these men were as little Gallic nationalists as Vindex had been. Julius Classicus had led the Vitellian advance as far as the Maritime Alps in early 69; the other leaders, Julius Tutor and Julius Sabinus, were 'Romans' to such an extent that Dillius Vocula's legions accepted their command after the disastrous retreat from Vetera. In the absence of any senator who might be put up as the Vitellians' candidate for the imperial office, Julius Sabinus made a bid by claiming that his grandfather had been an illegitimate son of none other than Julius Caesar himself. The 'Gallic Empire' (*Imperium Gallianum*) which they called for was not an empire controlled by the Gauls, but a Roman empire in Gaul.

The lack of a plausible leader and the appearance of Cerealis in the lower Rhineland made it clear to the legionaries that – after Cerealis himself had rejected an offer to be their emperor – there was no alternative to accepting Vespasian. The Flavians did what they could to win the loyalty of these supporters of Vitellius. The next years saw major military activity in Britain under Cerealis and (from 78) Agricola, to give the legions there the chance to win honour as soldiers of Vespasian. Their conditions were improved by the construction of more permanent, stone camps. And the story of their war against Civilis was re-written to make it seem that they had always been loyal to Rome, fighting German barbarians and Celtic and Batavian traitors. Unlike Galba, Otho or Vitellius, Vespasian managed to win the support even of those who had fought against him. The new dynasty was accepted as the legitimate successor of the Julio-Claudians.

Fig. 22. Gold aureus, AD 71 (Lyon). Vespasian, holding palm-branch and sceptre, celebrates his triumph over Judaea; there is a trumpeter behind, and his chariot is preceded by a soldier holding a captive.

Suggestions for Further Study

1. 'At Rome, the consuls, the Senate, and the equestrians rushed headlong into servitude' (Tacitus, *Annals* I,7). Was there any alternative in AD 14 to giving all of Augustus' powers to Tiberius?

2. Tacitus suggests that right from the beginning of his reign, Tiberius despised the Senate. Modern scholars have suggested that in fact he intervened too little in the affairs of the Senate, thus causing confusion by failing to make his own policies and intentions plain and allowing informers to lodge accusations of *maiestas*. Is Tacitus' picture fair, or was he reading back into the time of Tiberius the autocracy of Domitian and Hadrian in his own time?

3. Tacitus insists that Tiberius hated Germanicus and his children. How strong is the evidence that Tiberius was jealous of Germanicus? Did Tacitus build Germanicus up as a hero merely for literary reasons, as a foil to Tiberius?

4. Tiberius succeeded in persuading both contemporaries and later generations that Sejanus had plotted against him. Why were so many people at Rome prepared to believe that Sejanus threatened their well-being?

5. Several ancient writers tried to divide Caligula's reign into a 'good' beginning and a 'bad' end, but they could not agree on when the change came, or why. Do you think that such a division is valid? Did Caligula end up behaving like a madman?

6. Ancient sources suggest that Claudius' selection as emperor by the praetorian guard was a quirk of fortune. Was Claudius in fact Caligula's legitimate successor?

7. Is it valid to ascribe to Claudius a conscious programme of political and administrative reforms? Why did he invade Britain? Why did he extend civic rights to the Gauls?

8. 'Senators executed: 35; equestrians: 221; others, "as many as the grains of sand and dust"' (Seneca, *The Transformation of Claudius into a Pumpkin*, 14). Why were there so many conspiracies against Claudius? Were they real or imagined? Why did they cease after AD 49?

9. Roman law excluded women from public office. How, and to what extent, could women like Livia, Antonia the Younger, Messallina and Agrippina affect the course of political events?

10. Why did Nero fail when his reign began so auspiciously?

11. Some scholars believe that the German legions led by Verginius Rufus only engaged and defeated Vindex's levies at the Battle of Vesontio in AD 68 as the result of a mistake. Is this a plausible interpretation? Why is it so difficult to tell what Rufus' real intentions were?

12. Tacitus refers to Galba's 'long and bloody journey' from Spain to Rome. Why did he disappoint so many different groups of people so quickly? Should he have adopted Otho as his successor instead of Piso? Could Otho ever obtain legitimacy, having come to the throne through murder?

13. Tacitus' statement that the civil wars of AD 68-69 showed that 'an emperor could be made elsewhere than at Rome' has been interpreted to mean that Roman emperors needed nothing more than the support of a powerful provincial army. Does this explain why Nero, Galba, Otho and Vitellius failed, and Vespasian succeeded? Or would you rather agree with the view that the only first-century emperor whom one can properly describe as the candidate of his army was Vitellius?

14. The first person to announce his support for Vespasian in AD 69 was the Prefect of Egypt, Tiberius Julius Alexander; yet he was neither an Italian, nor a senator. Which groups of people in the Roman empire were responsible for ensuring that Vespasian became emperor? Might some other leader have replaced Vitellius?

15. Can we rely on Tacitus to present the reader with reliable characterisations of the political figures who appear in the *Annals* and *Histories*?

Suggestions for Further Reading

A. GENERAL

Political history

Many of the standard narratives covering this period take too little account of social institutions such as the *domus,* and of research on Roman social history since the 1960's. Good accounts available in English include A. Garzetti, *From Tiberius to the Antonines* (London, 1974); M. Grant, *History of Rome* (London, 1979); and H.H. Scullard, *From the Gracchi to Nero* (5th edn., London, 1982). C. Wells, *The Roman Empire* (Fontana, 1984) is more analytical. For biographies of the emperors, see M. Grant, *The Roman Emperors* (London, 1985); for the women of the imperial family, J.P.V.D. Balsdon, *Roman Women* (London, 1962), chs. 4 & 5, and N. Kokkinos, *Antonia Augusta: Portrait of a Roman Lady* (London, 1992). T.P. Wiseman (ed.), *Roman Political Life 90 BC-AD 69* (Exeter, 1985), stresses the continuity of values between republic and principate, and underemphasises the changes in the political system.

Social and political structures

P. Garnsey & R. Saller, *The Early Principate* (Greece & Rome *New Surveys in the Classics,* no.15, 1982); covered in greater detail in P. Garnsey & R. Saller, *The Roman Empire: Economy, Society and Culture* (London, 1987). On the emperor, his household, and his soldiers, see F. Millar, *The Emperor in the Roman World* (Oxford, 1977); P.R.C. Weaver, *Familia Caesaris* (Cambridge, 1972); J.B. Campbell, *The Emperor and the Roman Army* (Oxford, 1984). Other aspects of the life of the political class are treated in R.P. Saller, *Personal Patronage under the Early Empire* (Cambridge, 1982), R.J.A. Talbert, *The Senate of Imperial Rome* (Princeton, 1984) and R.J.A. Talbert (ed.), *Atlas of Classical History* (London, 1985).

Collections of source material

The most comprehensive collection of translations of original sources for this period is D. Braund, *Augustus to Nero: a Sourcebook* (London, 1985). Other useful sourcebooks are B.W. Jones & R.D. Milns, *The Uses of Documentary Evidence in the Study of Roman Imperial History* (Sydney, 1984); N. Lewis & M. Reinhold, *Roman Civilization* (2 vols, New York, 1966); and R.K. Sherk, *The Roman Empire: Augustus to Hadrian* (Translated Documents of Greece and Rome, 6: Cambridge, 1988). While these collections concentrate on epigraphic and numismatic material, some of them also have extracts from the literary sources.

The standard collections of documents in the original Latin or Greek relating to the political history of the period are V. Ehrenberg & A.H.M. Jones, *Documents illustrating the Reigns of Augustus and Tiberius* (Oxford, 1955); E.M. Smallwood, *Documents illustrating the Principates of Gaius Claudius & Nero* (Cambridge, 1967); and M. McCrum & A.G. Woodhead, *Documents of the Flavian Emperors* (Cambridge, 1961).

On the problems we face in trying to interpret the non-literary sources, see M. Crawford (ed.), *Sources for Ancient History* (Cambridge, 1983): ch. 2 (epigraphy), ch. 3 (archaeology), ch. 4 (numismatics); J. Casey, *Understanding Ancient Coins* (Batsford, 1986). C.H.V. Sutherland, *Roman History and Coinage, 44 BC-AD 69* (Oxford, 1987; pbk., 1988), has brief discussions of fifty separate historical problems illustrated by surviving coins.

The ancient historians

There are Penguin Classics translations of Tacitus' *Annals* and *Histories*; Suetonius' *The Twelve Caesars*; and Josephus' *Jewish War*. English translations of most other historians can be found the Loeb Classical Library. There is a Penguin Classics translation of books 51 to 56 of Cassius Dio, entitled *The Augustan Narrative*, and a selection from books 58-63 edited by J. Edmondson as *Dio: the Julio-Claudians* (*Lactor* 15, 1992). Plutarch's *Lives of Galba and Otho* is available in translation, with commentary, by Little & Ehrhardt (BCP, London 1994).

Useful for an understanding of these texts as literature are T.A. Dorey (ed.), *Latin Historians* (London, 1966); N.P. Miller 'Dramatic Speech in the Roman Historians', *Greece and Rome* 22 (1975), 45-57; A.J. Woodman, 'Reading the Ancient Historians', *Omnibus* 5, 24-7.

Information about other Latin writers of the period may be found in *The Cambridge History of Classical Literature*, vol.II pt. 4: *The Early Principate* (Cambridge, 1982). The *Oxford Classical Dictionary* (Oxford, 2nd edn., 1970; 3rd edn., forthcoming) is always worth referring to. On Tacitus, R. Syme, *Tacitus* (Oxford, 1958) remains the standard work (856 pages). A shorter study is B. Walker, *The Annals of Tacitus. A Study in the Writing of History* (Manchester, 1968). See also N.P. Miller, 'Tacitus' Narrative Technique', *Greece and Rome* 24 (1977), 13-22; J. Percival, 'Tacitus and the Principate', *Greece and Rome* 27 (1980), 119-133.

Other major authors are discussed in A. Wallace-Hadrill, *Suetonius* (London, 1983), and F. Millar, *A Study of Cassius Dio* (Oxford, 1964).

B. FOR PARTICULAR CHAPTERS

Chapters 4-7

Tiberius' reign is described by Tacitus in books I to VI of the *Annals* (the section describing the overthrow of Sejanus is lost), and by Cassius Dio in books 56, 29-58. There is also Suetonius' *Life*.

Inscriptions etc.: Braund 91-2 (earthquake in Asia), 95-103 (Sejanus), 109-11 (Drusus and Gemellus), 112-15, 120 (Germanicus' family); 295-6, 557-9 (Germanicus in Egypt); 379 (Blaesus in Africa); Sherk 28 (the *Fasti*), 33-4 (Germanicus in Greece and Egypt), 35 (control of games), 40 (Sejanus).

B.M. Levick, *Tiberius the Politician* (London, 1976)

R. Seager, *Tiberius* (London, 1972)

A.J. Woodman, *Velleius Paterculus: The Tiberian Narrative* (Cambridge, 1977)

P.A. Brunt, 'The role of the Senate in the Augustan regime', *Classical Quarterly* 34 (1984), 423-44

R.J.A. Talbert, 'Augustus and the Senate', *Greece & Rome* 31 (1984), 55-63

G.W. Houston, 'Tiberius on Capri', *Greece & Rome* 32 (1985), 176-96

R. Syme, 'Sejanus on the Aventine', *Hermes* 84 (1956), 257-66 = *Roman Papers* I (1979), 305-14

Chapters 8 & 9

Tacitus' narrative for this period is lost. We depend upon Cassius Dio 59, and Suetonius' *Life*. The minutes of meetings of the Arval Brethren are preserved for the period from January 38 to June 40 (Smallwood, nos. 1-11). Caligula's assassination and its aftermath are described by Josephus in his *Antiquities of the Jews*, 19, 248-73 (= Braund 195); this account maximises the role of Herod Agrippa, and seems to have been based on the history of a consular who laid inordinate emphasis on the events in the Senate. For the *Fasti*, see Sherk 28; also 41 (= Braund 563, oath of loyalty), 42 (client kings); Braund 175-80, 183 (coins), 187-8; 194 (Claudius' accession), 565-7 (Jews).

J.P.V.D. Balsdon, *The Emperor Gaius* (Oxford, 1934?)

A.A. Barrett, *Caligula* (London, 1989)

M.K. Thornton, 'Julio-Claudian Building Programs', *Historia* 35 (1986), 28-44

C.J. Simpson, 'The "conspiracy" of AD 39', *Studies in Latin Literature and Roman History* II (ed. C. Deroux, Brussels, 1980), 347-66

D. Fishwick, 'The Annexation of Mauretania', *Historia* 20 (1971), 467-87

M. Swan, 'Josephus *A.J.* xix 251-2: Opposition to Gaius and Claudius', *American Journal of Philology* 91 (1970), 149-64

Chapters 10 & 11

The period from 47 AD to the fall of Messallina is covered in what remains of Tacitus, *Annals* XI, and that of Agrippina in book XII; cf. Cassius Dio 60; Suetonius' *Life*. Claudius' insecurity is stressed by Seneca in his *Apocolocyntosis*.

Cf. Braund 196-8 (coins), 200-10, 210-16 (Britain and the *pomerium*), 218-23, 234 (Agrippina), 410 (Marcus Silanus), 815-17 (concern for the corn-supply). We also have the text of parts of some of Claudius' speeches: Braund 568-73; see M.T. Griffin, 'The Lyons Tablet and Tacitean Hindsight', *Classical Quarterly* 32 (1982), 404-18.

A. Momigliano, *Claudius* (Oxford, 1934)

B. Levick, *Claudius* (London, 1990)

B. Levick, 'Antiquarian or revolutionary? Claudius Caesar's Conception of his Principate', *American Journal of Philology* 99 (1978), 79-105

On executions: D. McAlindon, 'Senatorial Opposition to Claudius and Nero', and 'Claudius and the Senators', *American Journal of Philology* 77 (1956), 113-32, and 78 (1957), 279-86

B. Baldwin, 'Executions under Claudius', *Phoenix* 18 (1964), 39-48

On Claudius' freedmen: F. Millar, *The Emperor*, pp. 69 ff.

S.I. Oost, 'The Career of M. Antonius Pallas', *American Journal of Philology* 79 (1958), 113-39

Chapters 12 & 13

Tacitus, *Annals* XIII-XVI (the end of Nero's reign is lost); Dio 61-63.21; Suetonius, *Nero*

Inscriptions etc.: Braund 325-8 (Nero's accession), Sherk 74 (Aurelius Victor on the *quinquennium*); Braund 240-58 and Sutherland, chs. 35–40 (coins); Braund 259 and Sherk 69-70 (Piso's plot); Braund 261-66 and Sherk 71-3, 75, 78 (Nero in Greece); 77 (confiscations in Africa); 104 (posthumous popularity).

Nero has a tendency to attract biographers. The best historical analyses are M.T. Griffin, *Nero: The End of a Dynasty* (London, 1984), and B.H. Warmington, *Nero* (London, 1969). M. Grant, *Nero* (London, 1970), is well illustrated.

M.T. Griffin, *Seneca: A Philosopher in Politics* (Oxford, 1976)

N.P.Miller, *Tacitus Annals 14: A Companion* (BCP 1987)

T.K.Roper, 'Nero, Seneca and Tigellinus', *Historia* 28 (1979), 346–357

J.P.Sullivan, *Literature and Politics in the Age of Nero* (Cornell UP, 1985)

Chapters 14-18

For AD 68, Plutarch's *Galba* is the only coherent narrative. For AD 69, there are books I-III of Tacitus' *Histories*, as well as Plutarch's *Otho*. The events of AD 70 are described in *Histories* IV and what remains of V. There are also Suetonius' *Lives*. All are based on pro-Flavian sources.

For coins, cf. Sherk 79, Braund 288, 290, 291; Sutherland, *Roman History and Coinage*, chs. 41-6; the selection in McCrum and Woodhead is wider, but untranslated. Sherk 81 is the acclamation of Vespasian at Alexandria; Braund 293 = Sherk 82, the *Lex de Imperio Vespasiani*.

On Vesontio, see P.A. Brunt, 'The Revolt of Vindex and the Fall of Nero' *Latomus* 18 (1959), 531-59; J.L. Daley, 'Verginius at Vesontio', *Historia* 24 (1975), 75-100; B. Levick, 'L. Verginius Rufus and the Four Emperors', *Rheinisches Museum* 128 (1985), 318-46. K. Wellesley, *The Long Year AD 69* (London 1975, 2nd edn. Bristol, 1989), and P.A.L. Greenhalgh, *The Year of Four Emperors* (London, 1975), both emphasise the military events of that year; see also G.E.F. Chilver, *A Historical Commentary on Tacitus' Histories I and II* (Oxford, 1979).

On Vespasian's supporters, see G. Townend, 'Some Flavian Connections', *Journal of Roman Studies* 51 (1961), 54-62; R. Syme, 'The March of Mucianus', *Antichthon* 11 (1977), 76-92 = *Roman Papers* III (1984), 998-1013; J. Nicols, *Vespasian and the Partes Flavianae* (Wiesbaden, 1976).

A biography of Vespasian by B. Levick is forthcoming.

List of Latin Terms

amicitia, amicus ('friendship', 'friend'): At Rome, as in many societies, friendship is a formal social institution. A man has the obligation to help his friends, and to listen to their advice: thus the emperor must show favour (*gratia*) to his friends, and accept the advice of those he has invited to his *consilium*. Conversely, he has the right to their trust: anyone accused of treason against the emperor, whether guilty or not (as Roman lawyers point out), can no longer be an *amicus* of the emperor. When the emperor's *amicitia* was formally revoked, the person concerned had either to go into exile or kill himself (like Cornelius Gallus, Piso or Seneca).

consilium: The semi-formal group of *amici* whose advice a Roman was bound to take. The Senate served this function for magistrates (including the emperor, who also had his domestic *consilium*).

consul (abbr. 'cos.'): The pair of magistrates who, under the republic, held supreme power. The *consules ordinarii* gave their names to the year in which they held office. If one or both died or resigned, they were succeeded by *consules suffecti*. Vitellius had himself appointed *consul perpetuus* (perpetually, i.e. for life), a post which both Augustus and Nero had rejected.

domus Caesaris: 'Household of Caesar', i.e., not just the emperor and his near relatives, but all the slaves and freedmen belonging to him, and by extension client kings as well as Roman *amici* who regarded themselves as dependants of the emperor.

equestrian order: Formally, the cavalry arm of the Roman army; in practice, the term was applied to all wealthy landowning citizens ('gentry', we might say) who were not members of the Senate.

freedmen (*liberti*): At Rome, slaves who had been set free became citizens, and could thus be used to perform administrative duties on their ex-master (patron)'s behalf. Under Claudius, the freedmen responsible for the emperor's accounts (*a rationibus*), correspondence (*ab epistulis*) and replies to requests (*a libellis*) were particularly influential.

imperium: The constitutional right, granted by election or by an extraordinary vote of the Roman people, to command in war; it was held by consuls and praetors. The commander was an *imperator*, whence our word 'emperor'; an emperor was acclaimed as such at his accession, and then again when one of his legates won a military victory.

legate: Roman magistrates might delegate their *imperium* to others. Thus the emperor governed different provinces through his legates.

liberti, see freedmen.

maiestas: The technical term for 'treason' was 'attempting to diminish the greatness (*maiestas*) of the Roman people'. From Augustus on, opposition to the emperor was included under this charge.

paterfamilias: The head of a Roman household. As the man who gave life to the entire state, and ensured its survival, the emperor was acclaimed as *pater patriae*, 'Father of the community' (Tiberius rejected the title).

pomerium: The ritual boundary of the city of Rome.

pontifex: One of the groups of state priests. The emperor was always Chief Priest, *pontifex maximus*.

possessio: A form of ownership in Roman law (see ch. 4).

potestas: Social power or authority (not including the power to command soldiers), e.g. that of a father over his household (*patriapotestas*), or that of the Tribunes (protectors) of the People. This tribunician *potestas* was one of the ways in which Roman emperors emphasised their role as protectors of ordinary citizens: thus St. Paul as a Roman citizen could appeal to Nero against the judgement of the governor of Judaea.

praetor: The second most senior annual magistracy. The main function of the praetors was administering justice.

prefect (*praefectus*): A Roman magistrate could appoint someone to exercise command on his behalf. Men 'put in charge' (*praefecti*) in this way included the commander of the general's bodyguard (*praefectus praetorio*, Praetorian Prefect) and the commander of the commissariat (*praefectus castrorum*). The emperor appointed a Prefect of Egypt, and prefects of the two fleets stationed at Misenum and Ravenna. These were equestrian; there were also senatorial prefects responsible for the corn supply (*praefecti frumenti dandi*), and a senior senator was appointed City Prefect (*praefectus urbi*). Once a year a junior member of the imperial family might be especially honoured by being appointed 'Prefect of the City for the Duration of the Latin Festival'.

princeps iuventutis: Augustus encouraged organised military training for young citizens (*iuventus*, 'youth'). The emperor's son was often honoured by being made the 'leader of youth'.

proconsul: A provincial governor with the powers of a consul. Under the principate, the term referred only to the governors of Asia and Africa, which were reserved for senior ex-consuls.

procurator: A wealthy Roman might appoint someone (normally a freedman) to look after his affairs on his behalf. Emperors had procurators to look after groups of estates, collect particular taxes, or even govern smaller provinces such as Palestine.

quaestor: A junior magistrate, normally in his early twenties, who would assist magistrates with *imperium* in matters of administration (especially finance).

recusatio imperii: The ritual whereby someone about to be acclaimed emperor pretends that he does not want to accept the office (the French term *refus de pouvoir* is often used).

senator: A member of the supreme council at Rome, whose collective advice was authoritative for magistrates (including, in principle, the emperor). From Augustus on, senators, their wives, children and grandchildren, formed a separate class (*ordo*, 'order') with special privileges.